Hey There BUILDER!

If you wanna listen to the gnarly audio narration of this book while you build your bridges, just scan the QR code here or follow this link
bit.ly/HowToBuildABridge

BOOKS THAT MAKE YOU SMILE

"I would like to dedicate this
book to my belly button, thanks
for always being there!"

-Albert B. Squid

SQUARE ROOT OF SQUID
PUBLISHING

HEY YOU!!!

So you like bridges? Of course you do, 'cause they are RAD. Engineers design all kinds of cool bridges from suspension, cable stay, truss, cantilever, arch, yadi yadi ya... the list goes on and on. In this book you will be able to not only build your own bridges, but will be able to test them as well. Find out how bridges are built from techniques to materials, while you build them yourself (out of paper, of course).

ALSO...

SAVE THE SCRAP PAPER

(why? it's a surprise, you will find out at the end)

WHAT YOU NEED

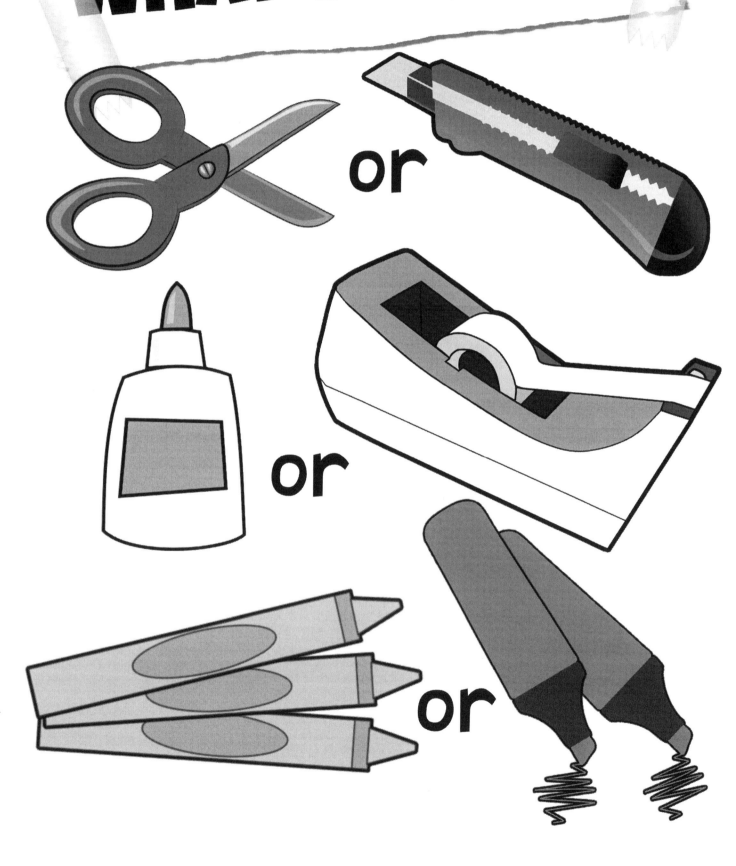

or

or

or

WARREN TRUSS BRIDGE

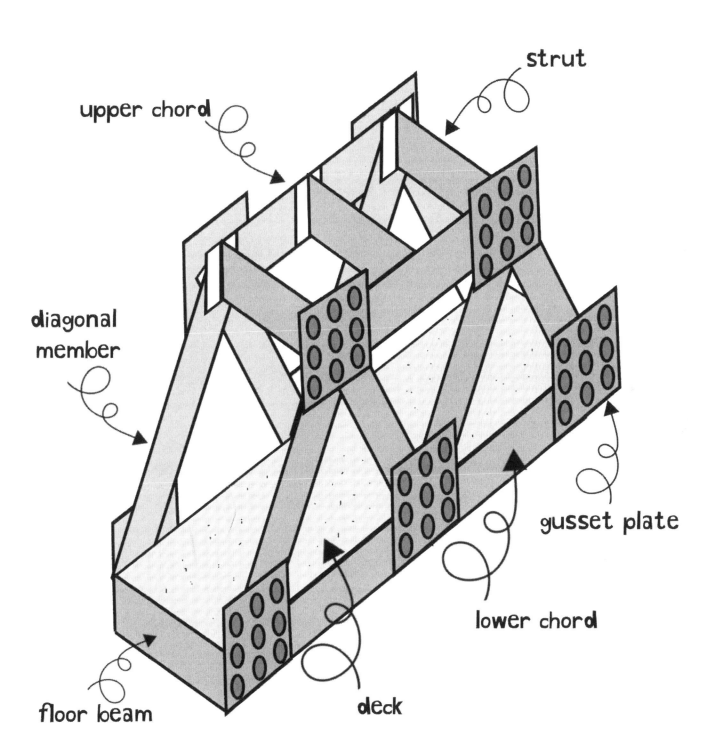

strut

upper chord

diagonal
member

gusset plate

lower chord

floor beam

deck

Why is the Warren Truss bridge so strong?

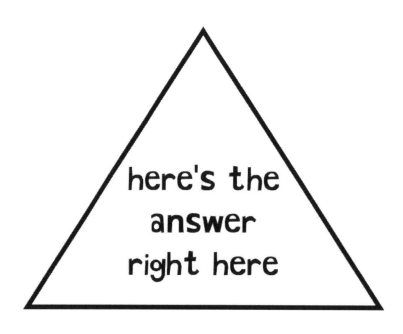

here's the
answer
right here

Our buddy the triangle!! When you push down on top of the triangle all the weight gets divided up instead of being all in one place. Think about it like this....you are holding up a big log over your head, (heavy right?) But then, five of your friends hold it up with you, (not so heavy anymore). That's what a triangle does in a bridge. So, guess what happens when you put a bunch of triangles together like in the Warren bridge? SUPER STRONG!

So, to start a bridge, Engineers will calculate what they need and then factories will make the parts usually of steel and concrete. This is our factory, so let's start making the parts (out of paper). Let's start with the bottom part of our bridge.

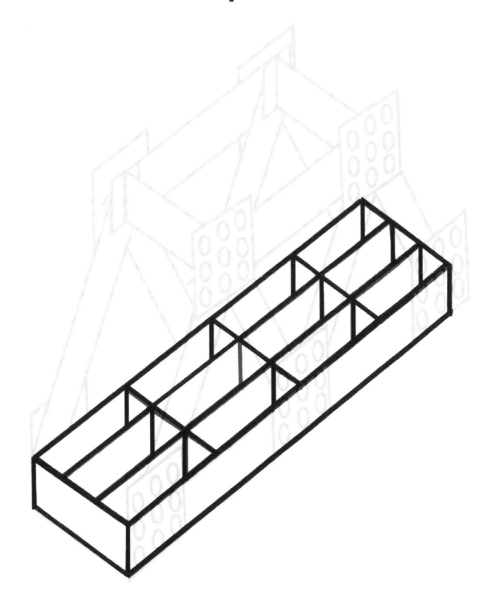

Cut out, fold, and glue
lower chords **1** & **2**
until each is flat.

1.

Cut out, fold, and glue
end beams **1** & **2** until
each is flat. Then fold
over end flaps.

end flaps

2.

Glue end beams to
lower chords with the
tabs.

3.

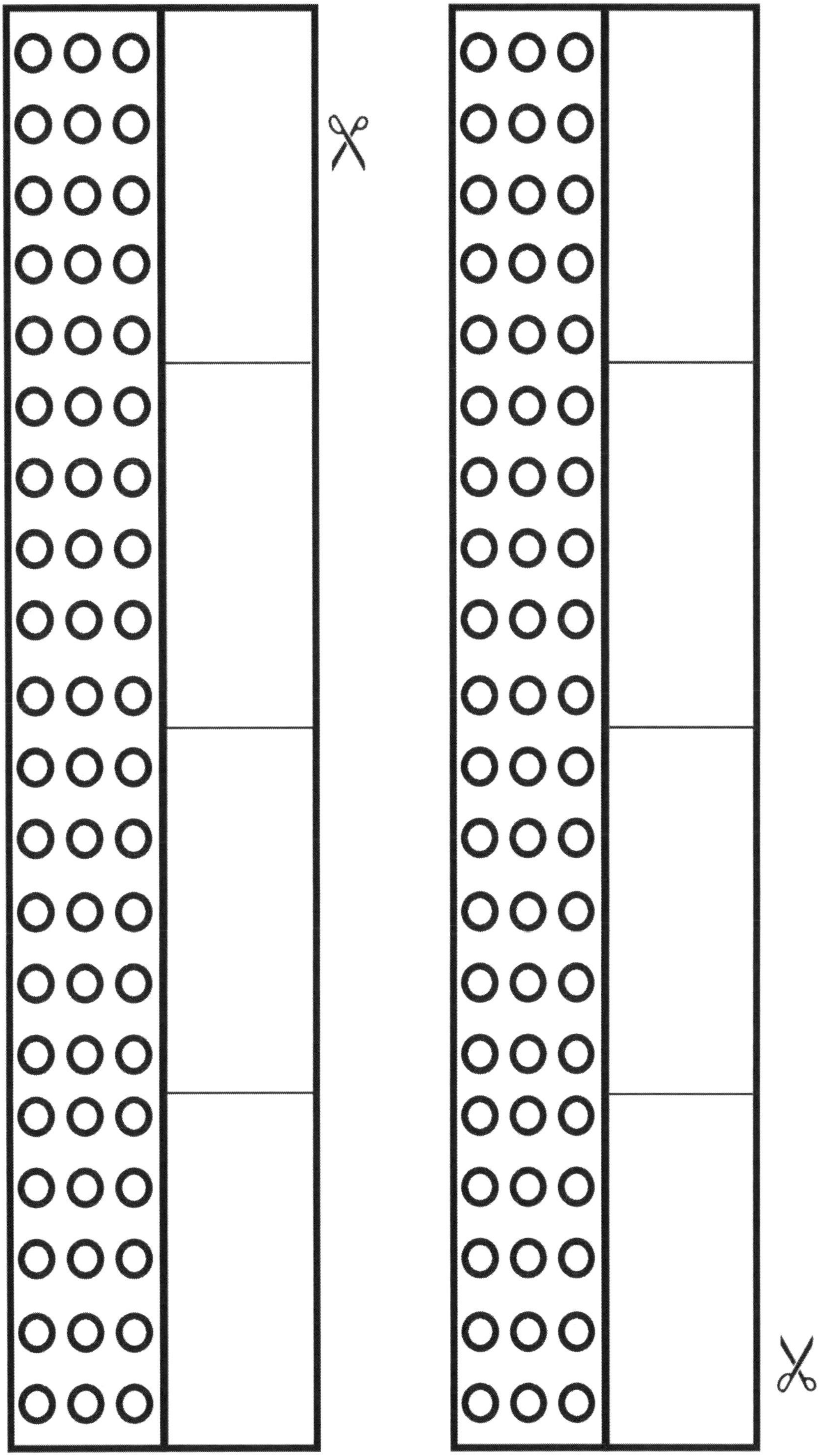

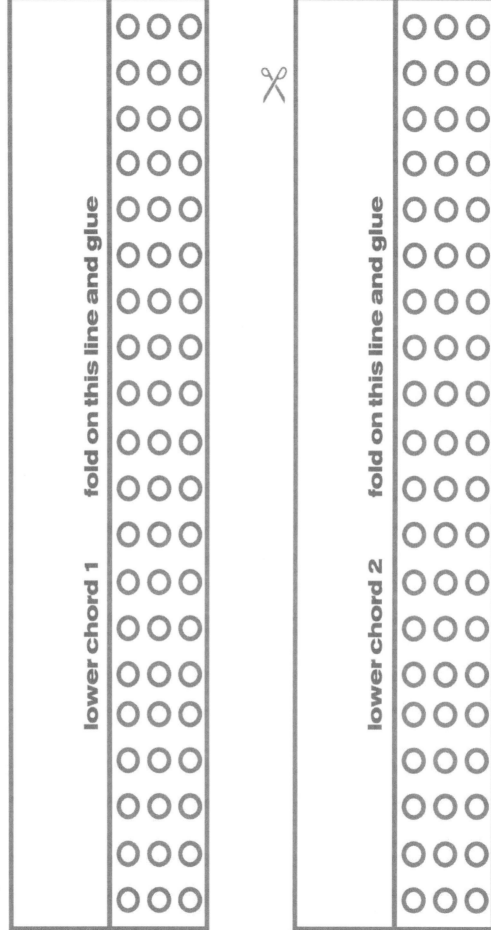

fold on this line and glue

lower chord 1

fold on this line and glue

lower chord 2

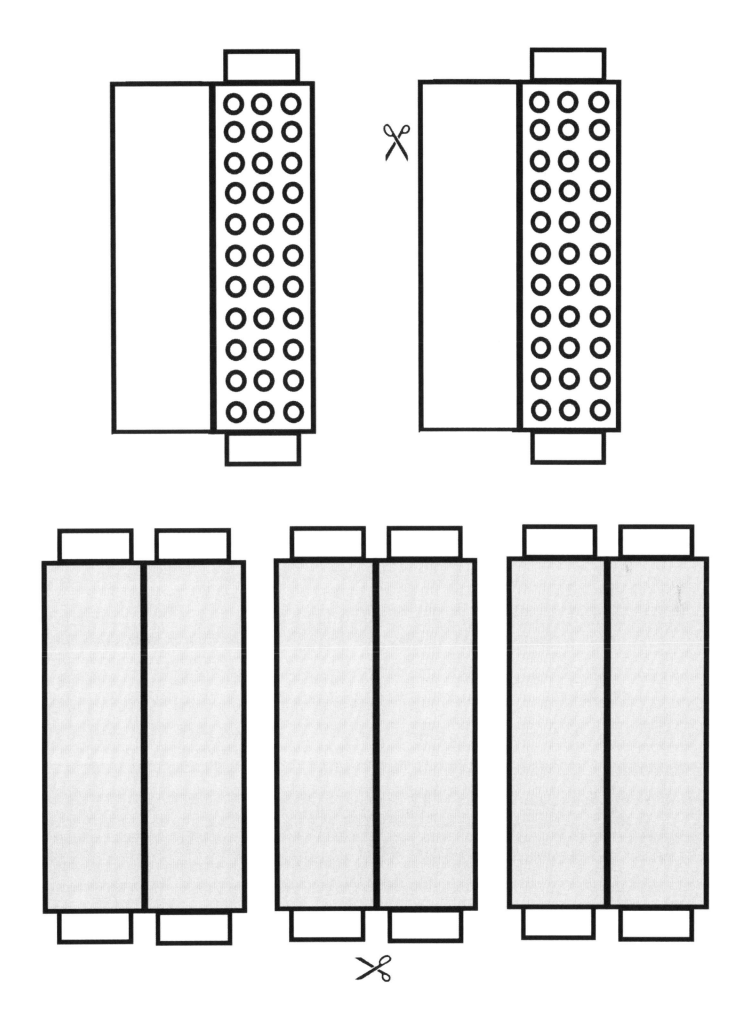

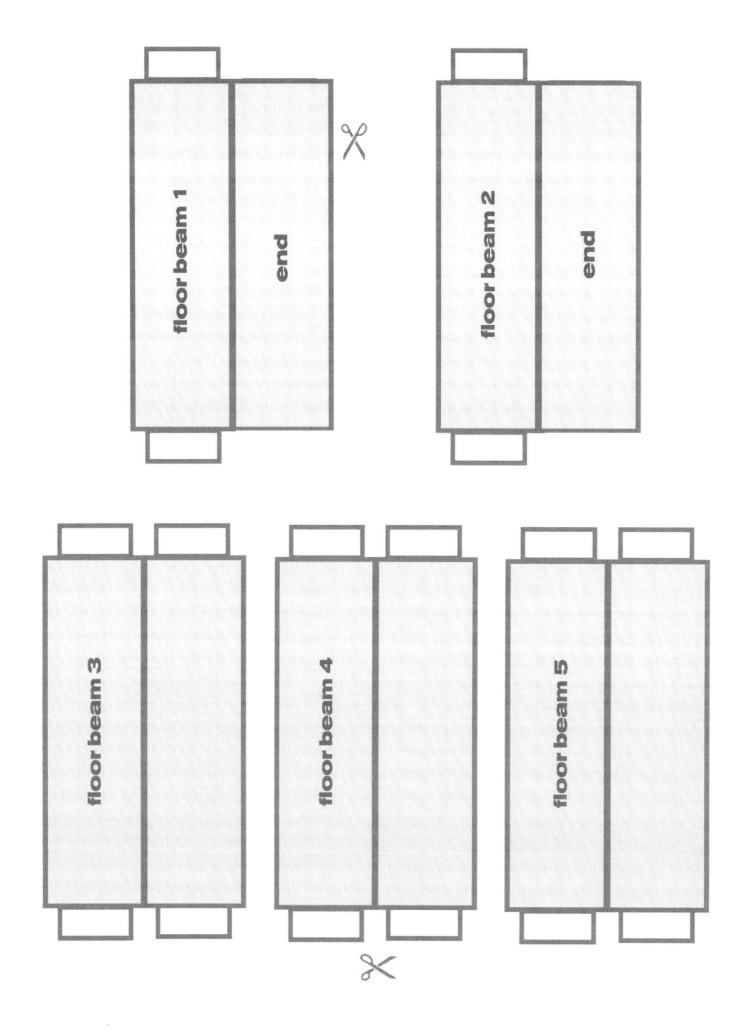

BRIDGE CONNECTIONS

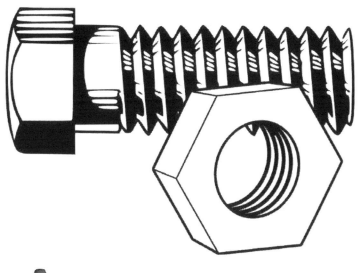

NUTS & BOLTS

Along with welding, nuts & bolts are the most efficient way to put a bridge together.

WELDING

Most metal bridges today are put together using the welding method. Bridge welders get paid BIG BUCKS too !

RIVETS

These guys are not used so much today. In the past most metal bridges were made with rivets.

(our bridge is paper, so we will connect it with glue!)

1.

Cut out, fold, and glue beams **1**, **2**, & **3** and fold flaps out.

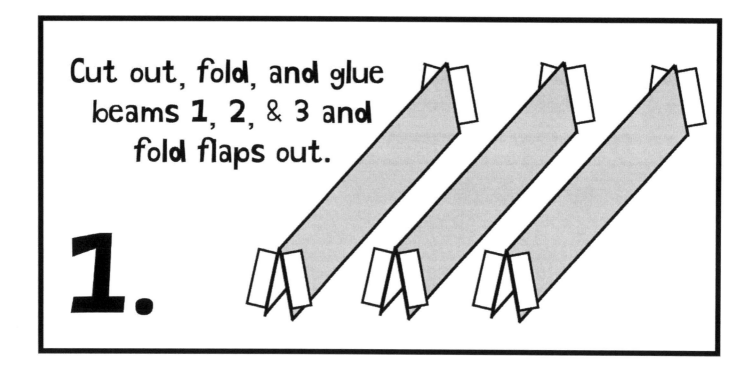

2.

Cut out, fold, and glue stringers **1** to **8** until each is flat. Then fold over end flaps.

Glue in the three beams on the lines first. Next, glue in the eight stringers.

floor beams

stringers

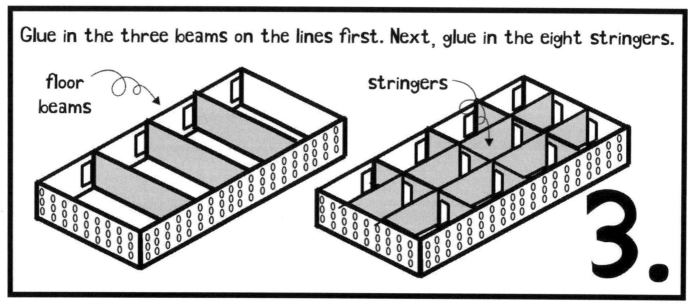

3.

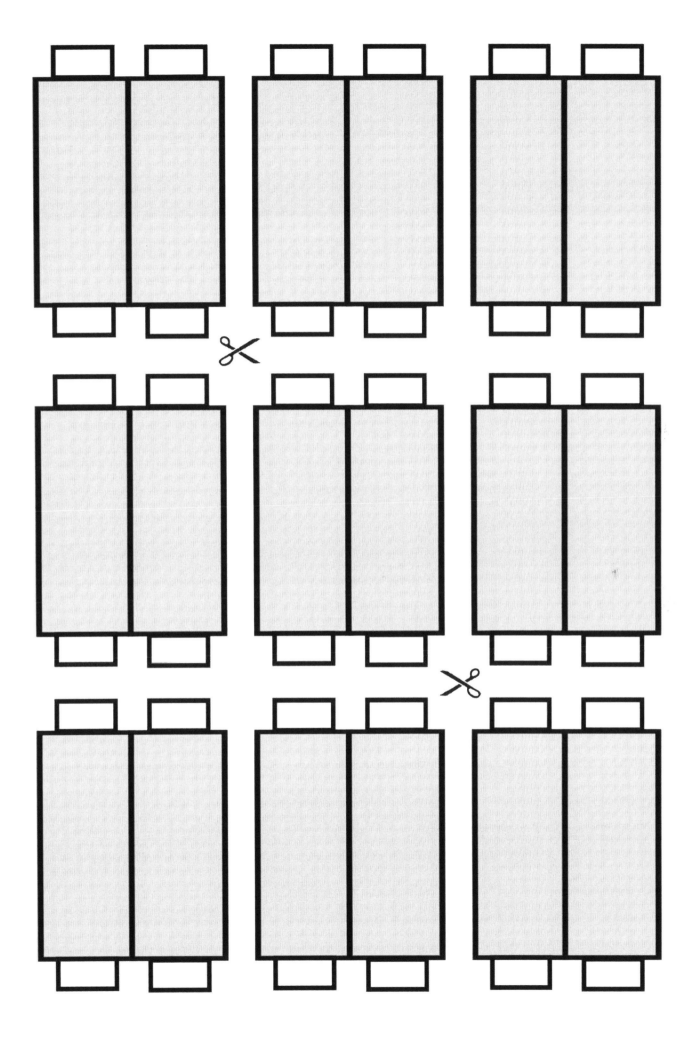

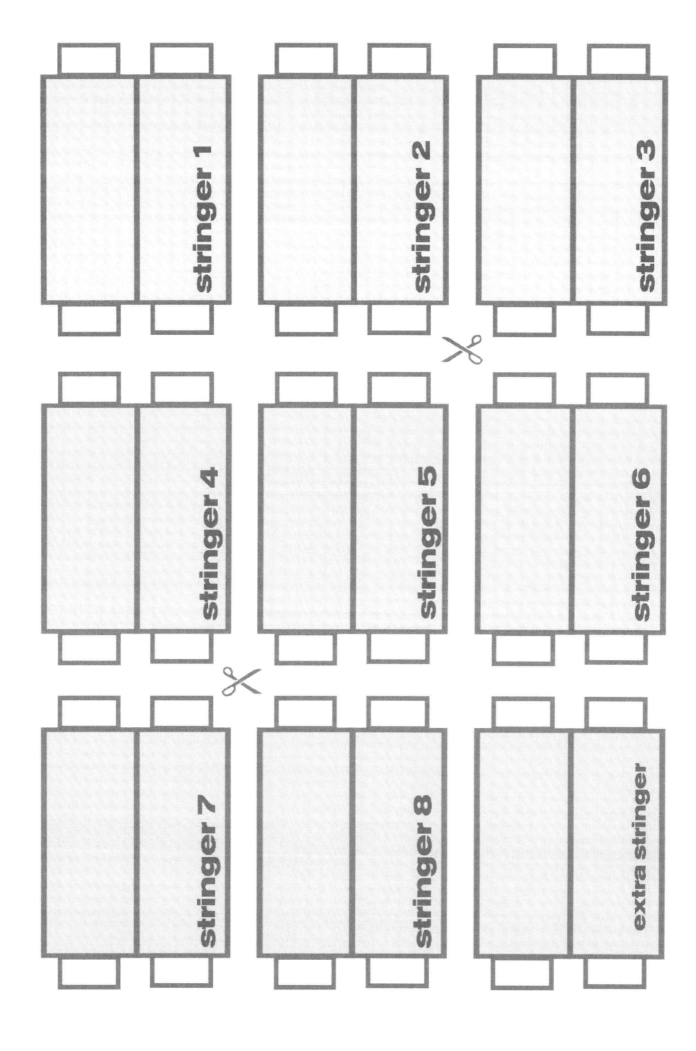

THE DECK

Truss bridges are very strong. The are often used for heavy trains to cross where tracks would be put over the floor beams. If it will be used for people and vehicles, a concrete deck is used. That's what we're gonna use.

(Our deck is made of paper, but you get the idea. Turn the page to find out how to apply the deck!)

1.

Cut out, fold, and glue the deck flat.

2.

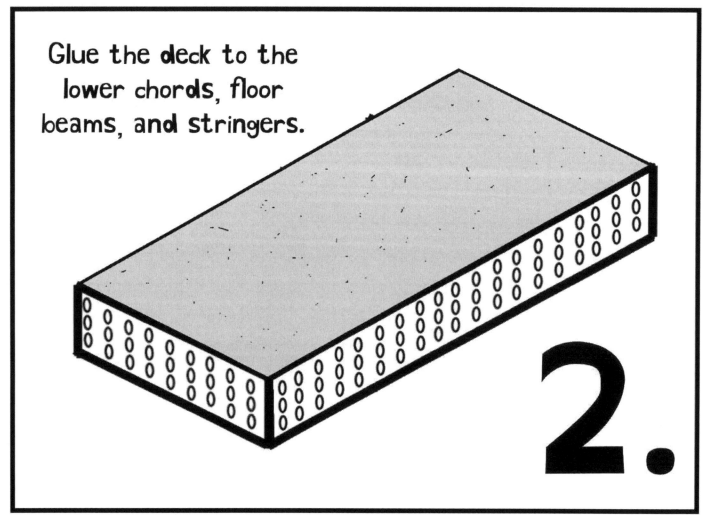

Glue the deck to the
lower chords, floor
beams, and stringers.

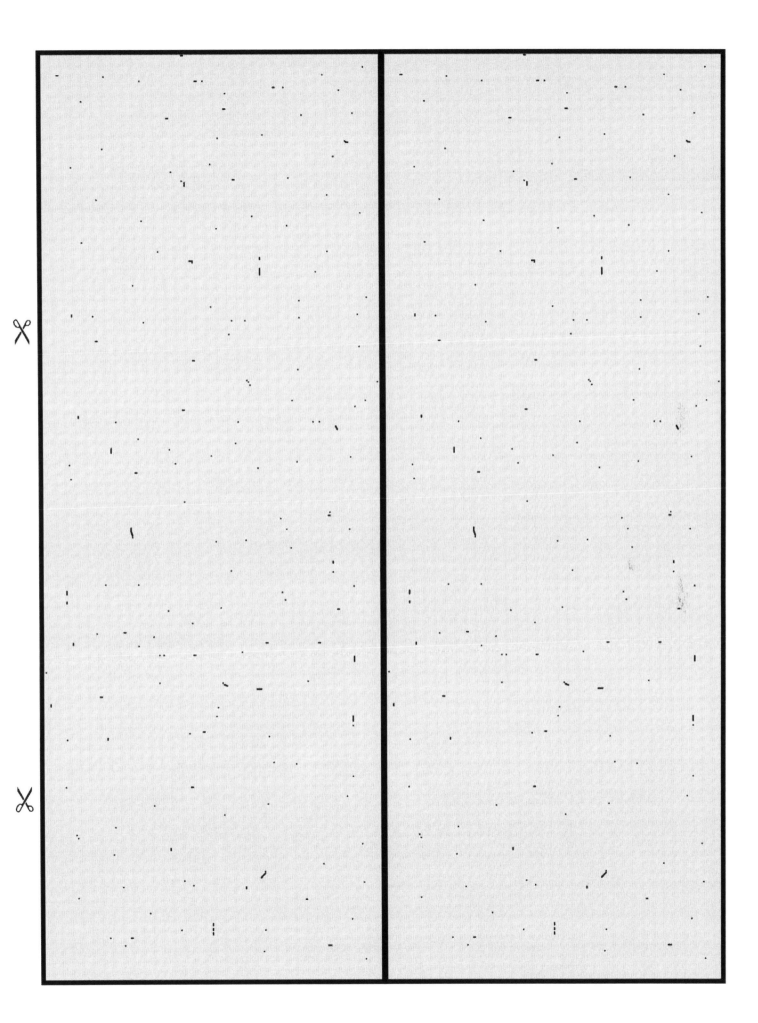

bridge deck --- fold on this line and glue

THE STEEL BEAMS

One of the most used materials for truss bridges is the steel I Beam. These guys make the lower and upper chords, the diagonals, and vertical parts of a truss bridge. Other types of steel beams used are box beams and plate beams.

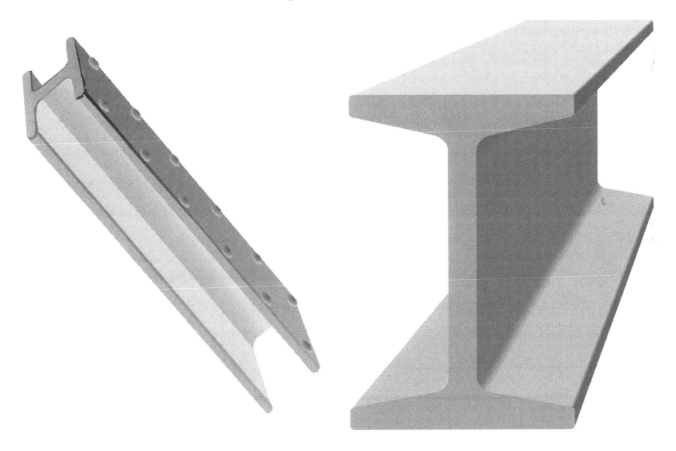

(Our paper I beams won't look like this, but they will get the job done for our model truss bridge!)

1.

Cut out, fold, and glue diagonal beams 1-8 until each is flat.

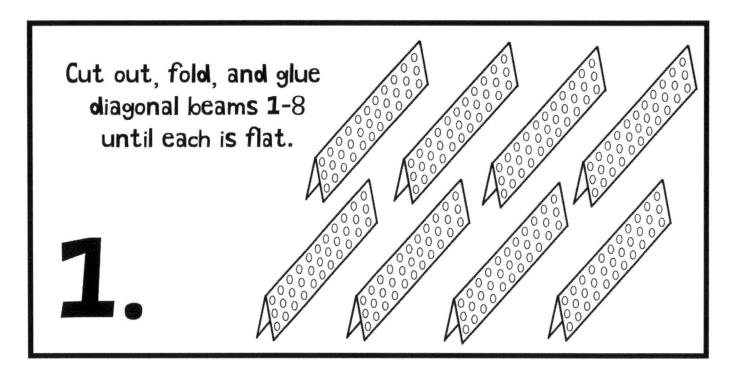

2.

Cut out, fold, and glue upper (top) chords and struts.

3.

Glue on the diagonals first, then glue on the upper chords and struts.

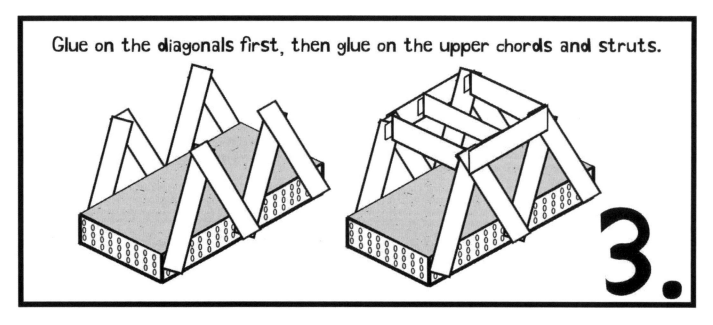

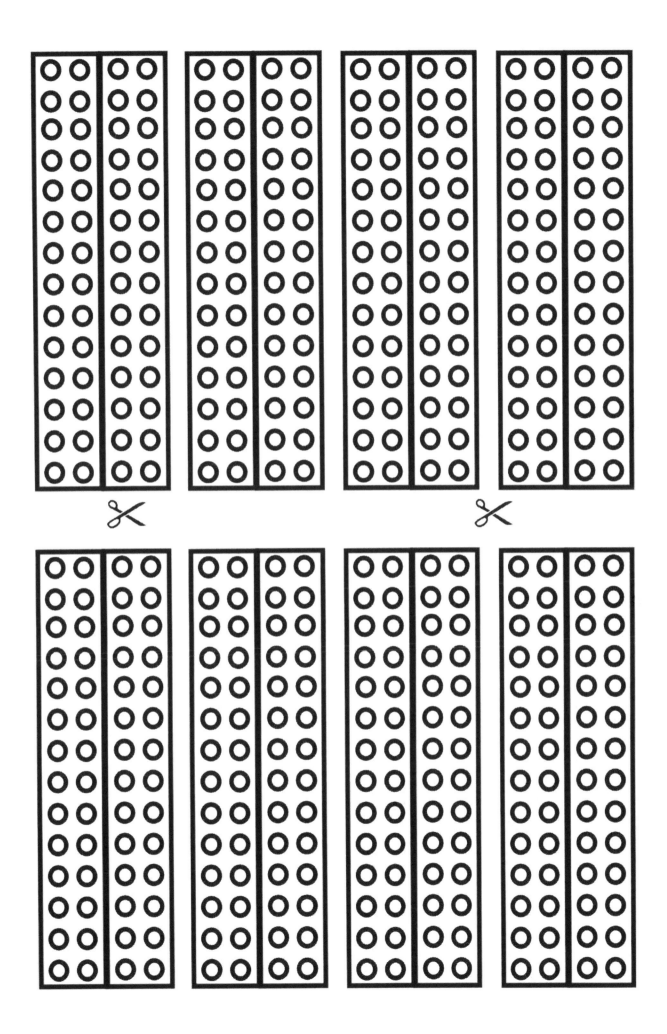

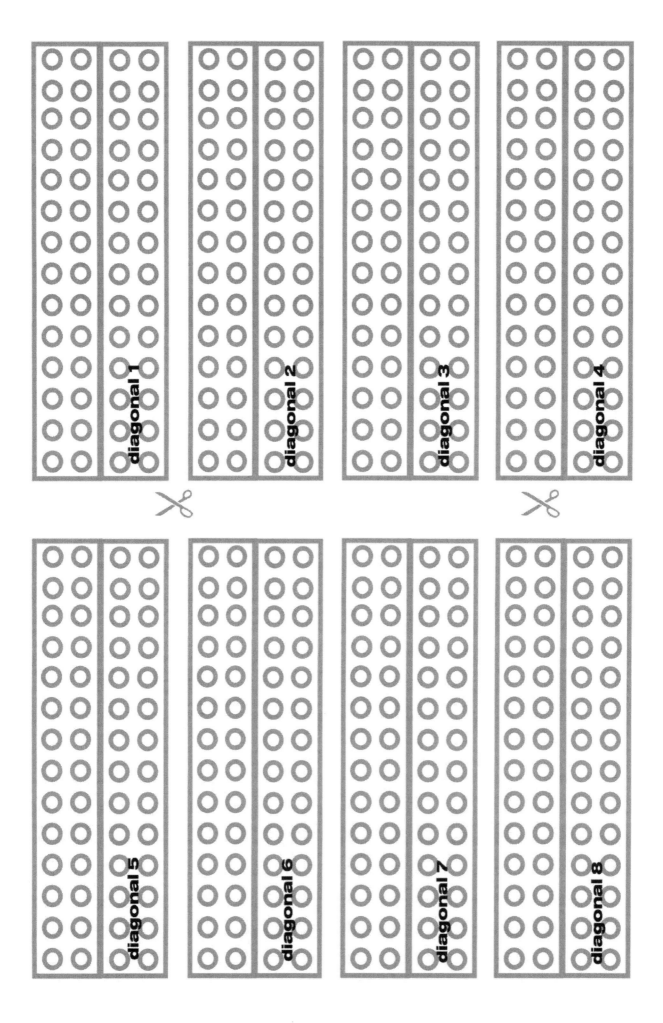

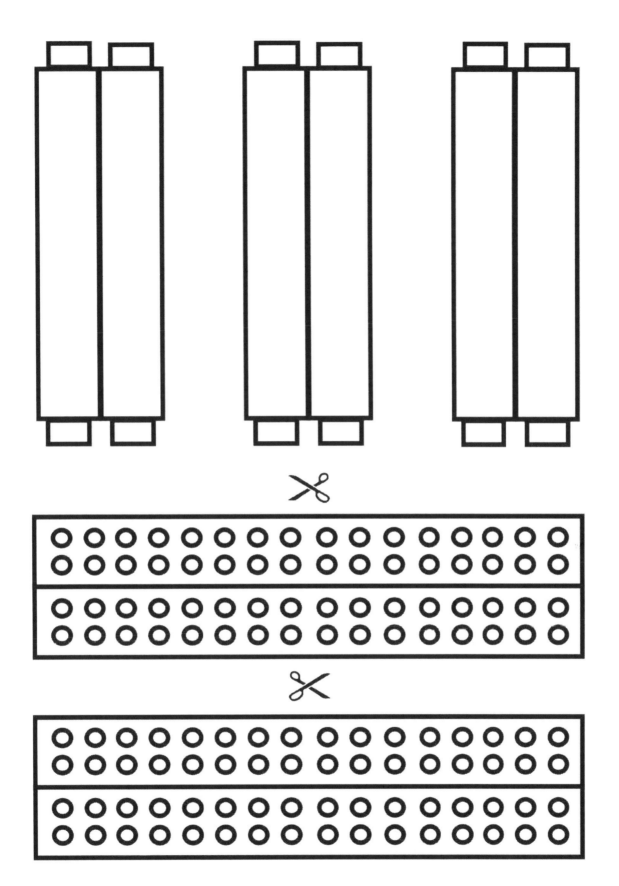

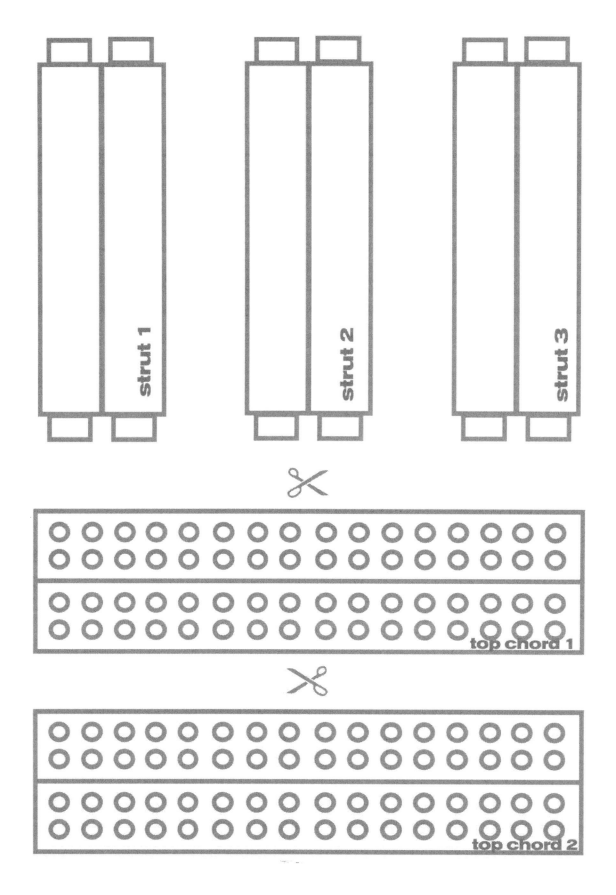

strut 1

strut 2

strut 3

top chord 1

top chord 2

THE GUSSET PLATES

These are the guys that tie everything together. Gusset plates are either **welded**, bolted, or riveted at the areas where the beams, diagonals, chords, and struts all meet each other.

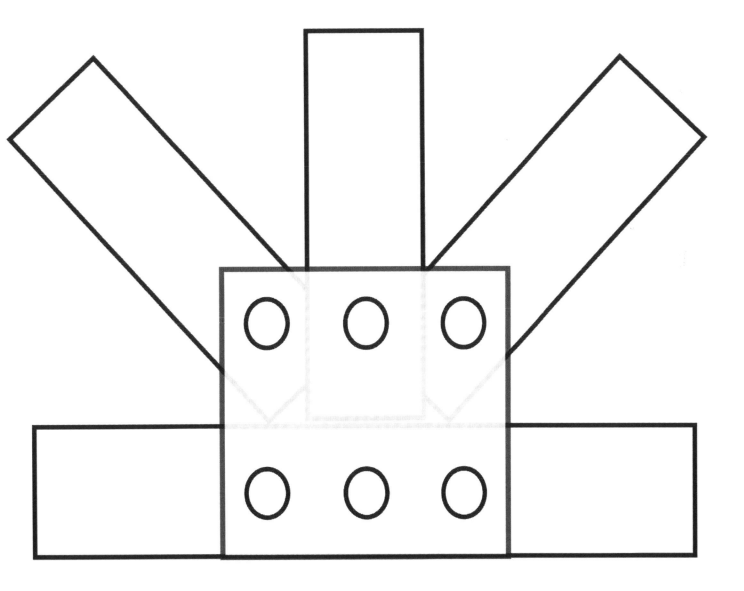

Put the gusset plates at all the places that meet.

1.

Cut out ten gusset plates from the following pages and glue 'em on the bridge.

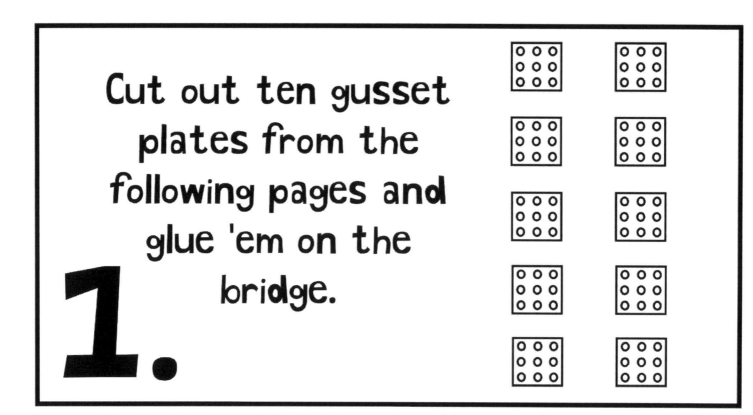

Some paint might look nice on this bridge!

2.

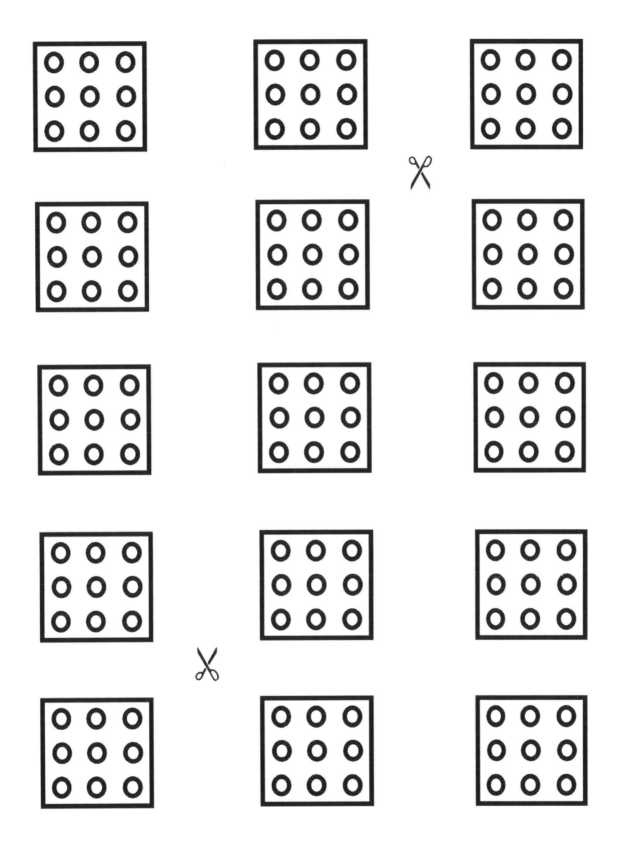

gusset plates

BEAM BRIDGE

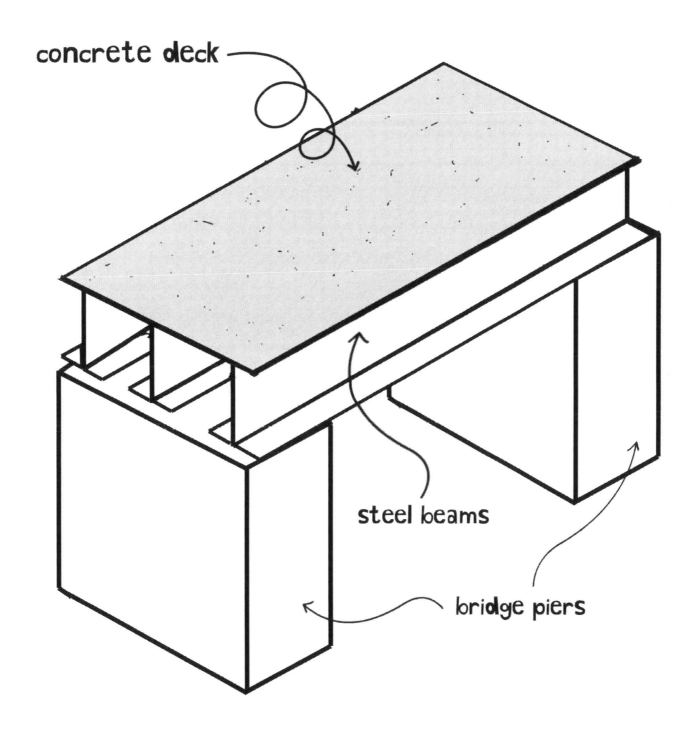

concrete deck

steel beams

bridge piers

(piled up books will make great piers for our paper beam bridge.)

What is a beam bridge?

A beam bridge is the most simple of all the bridges. It is just a horizontal thingy with two vertical thingies holdin' it up on both sides. These kind of bridges are used for things that are not that heavy.

Most modern beam bridges are made of steel beams, but in our case, paper will work.

TYPES OF BEAMS

I BEAMS

Can you see the letter "I"? These steel guys are used a lot in bridges.

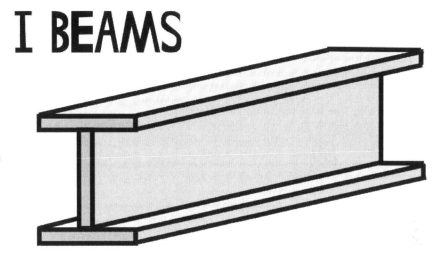

BOX BEAMS

These guys are usually made in a factory. There is a **square** hole in the middle. Makes sense they are called box beams.

PLATE BEAMS

These are cousins of the I Beam but they are made by **welding** a bunch of steel plates together.

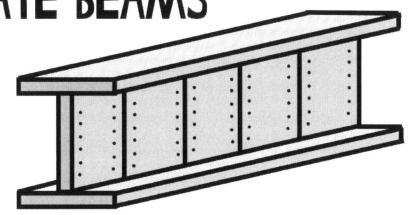

Fold and glue into a "T" shape.

1.

Glue two "T" shapes together to make one I Beam.

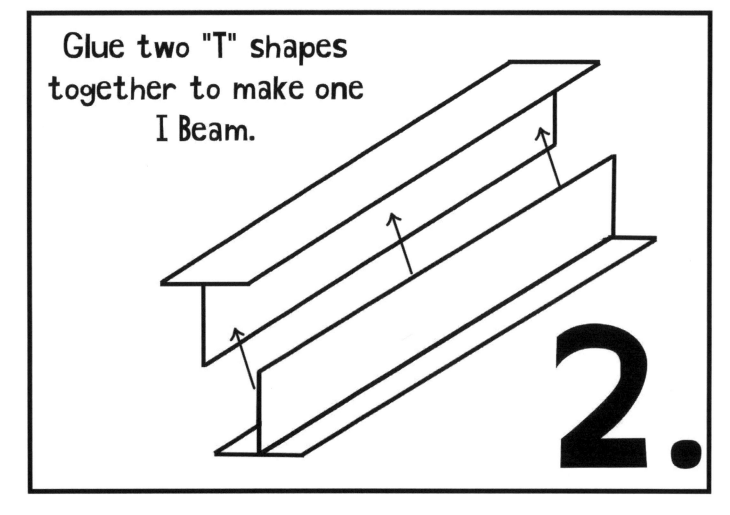

2.

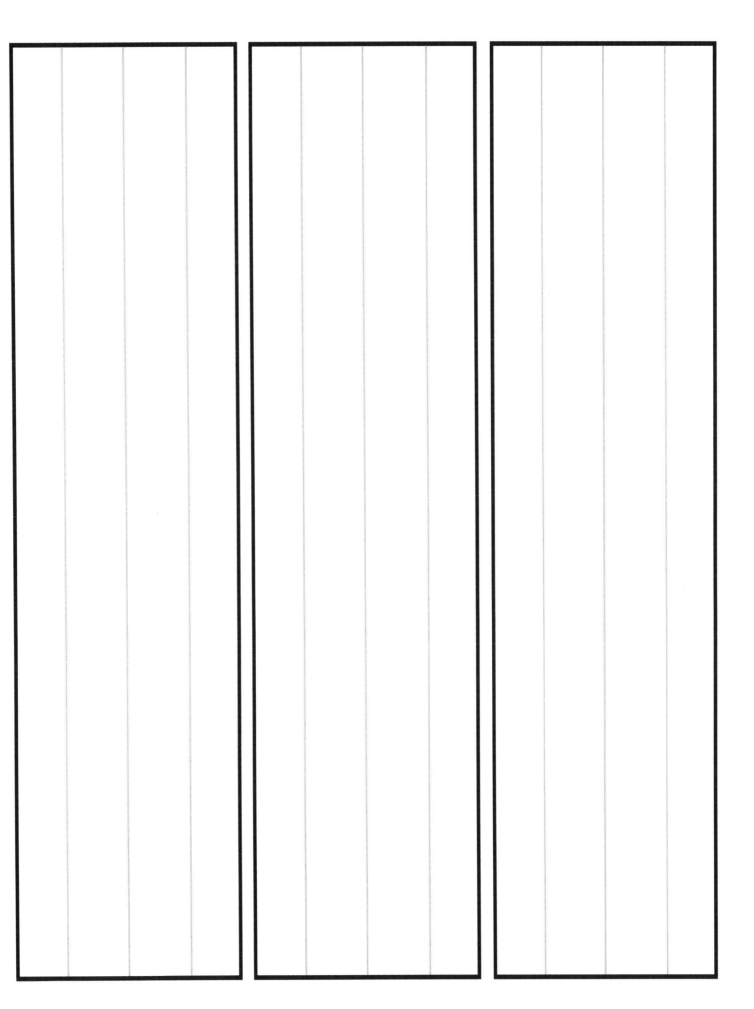

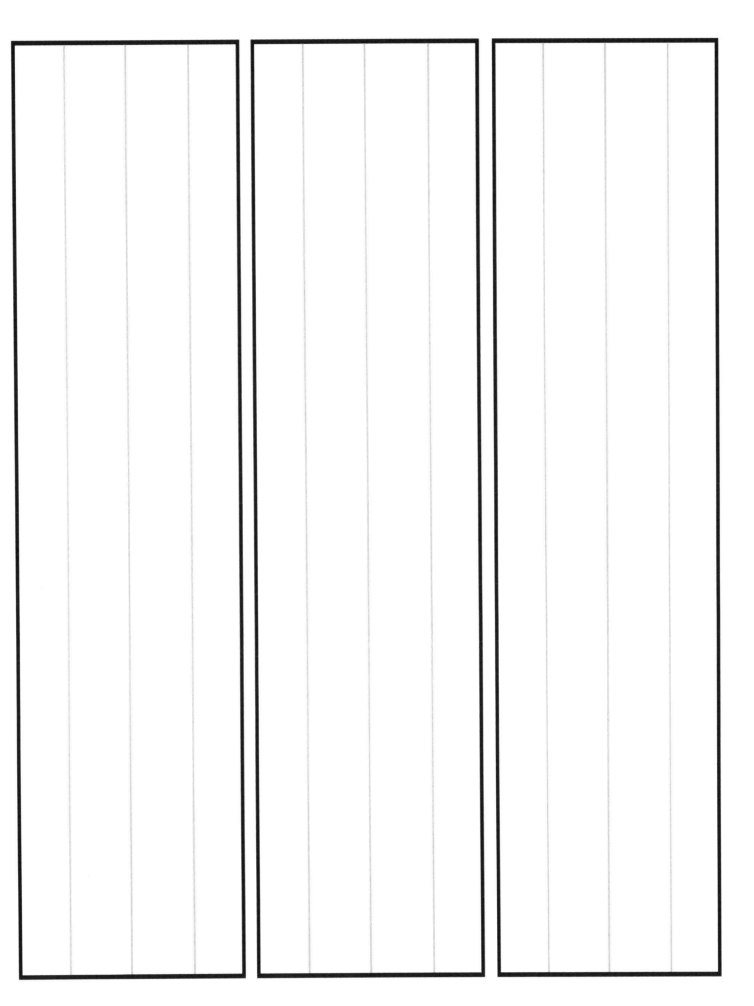

SUPER HERO ENGINEERS

Bridge Engineers really are super heroes 'cause they fight the EVIL forces of compression and tension when they design bridges. Whoa!!! That's crazy!!! WAIT!!! What IS "compression" and "tension" anyway?

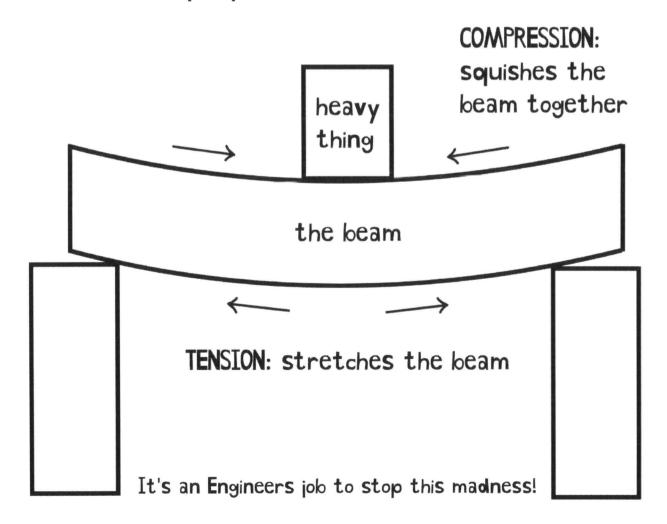

COMPRESSION: squishes the beam together

heavy thing

the beam

TENSION: stretches the beam

It's an Engineers job to stop this madness!

1.

Cut out, fold, and glue the deck flat.

2.

Glue the three beams on the lines provided on the bottom of the deck.

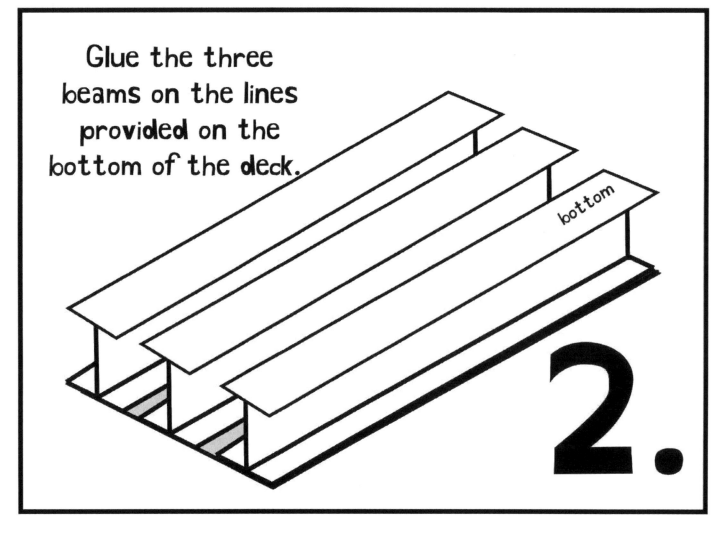

bottom

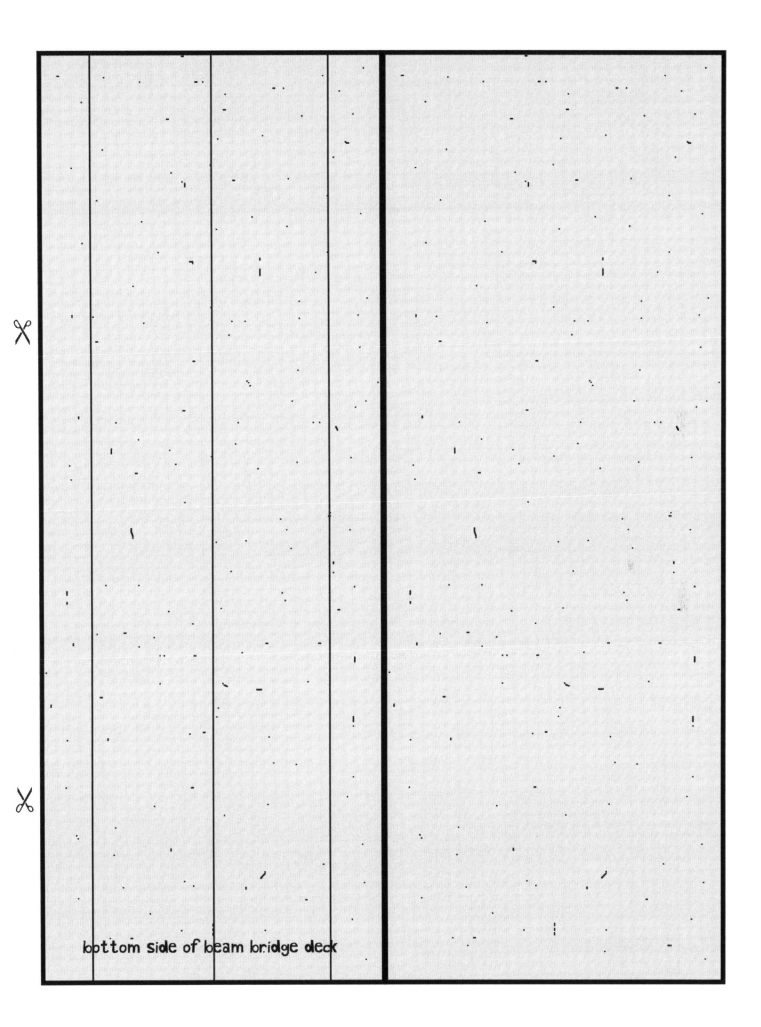

bottom side of beam bridge deck

bridge deck - - - fold on this line and glue

THE ARCH BRIDGE

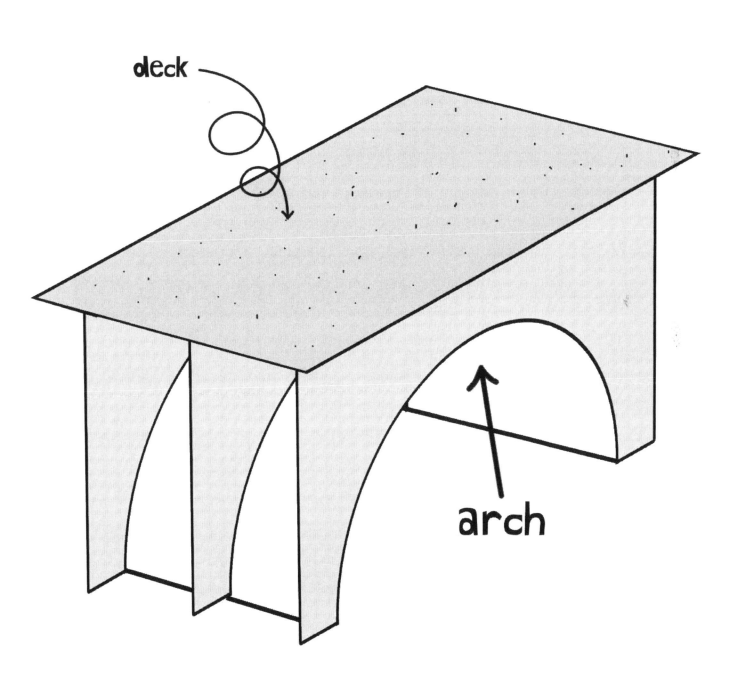

deck

arch

How do you build an arch?

Well, it wasn't easy, let me tell ya! In the old days they would make arch bridges out of stone. So, they would start from each side and build toward the middle. They would use a wooden frame to support the stones until they met at the middle. Once they got to the middle, they added a keystone that would make the arch strong, then take out the wooden frame (without the keystone and wooden frame, it would fall down). Some of these arches didn't even need mortar to stick 'em together and they are still standing today! They looked cool, but no need for stone arch bridges anymore, 'cause we have STEEL!!!

What makes an arch bridge strong?

The **difference** with an arch bridge from other bridges is that when a heavy weight is put on top, the whole bridge pushes out against the sides that the bridge is in between. So, instead of putting all the weight on piers going straight **down**, it spreads it out.

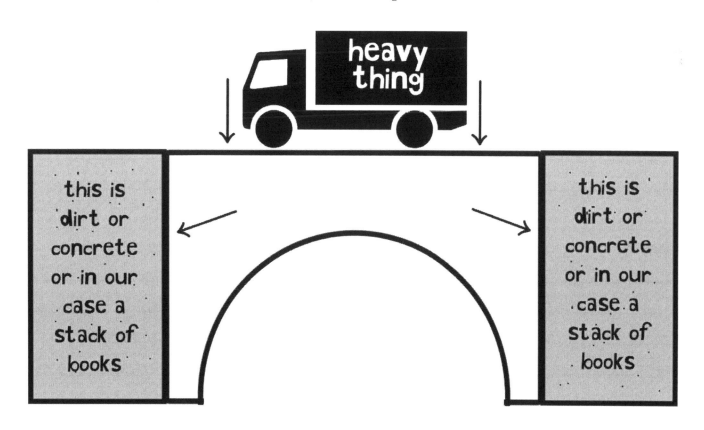

Fold and glue the three arches like this.

1.

Glue the three arches to the bottom of the road deck.

2.

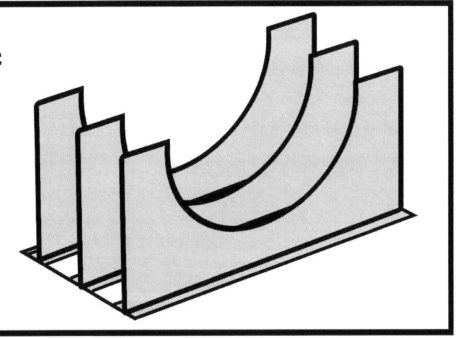

Glue in the arch curve.

3.

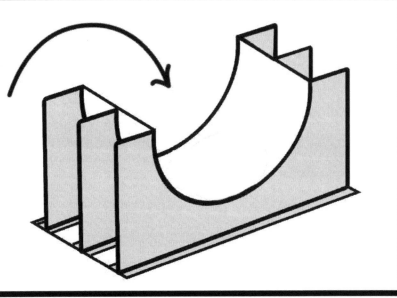

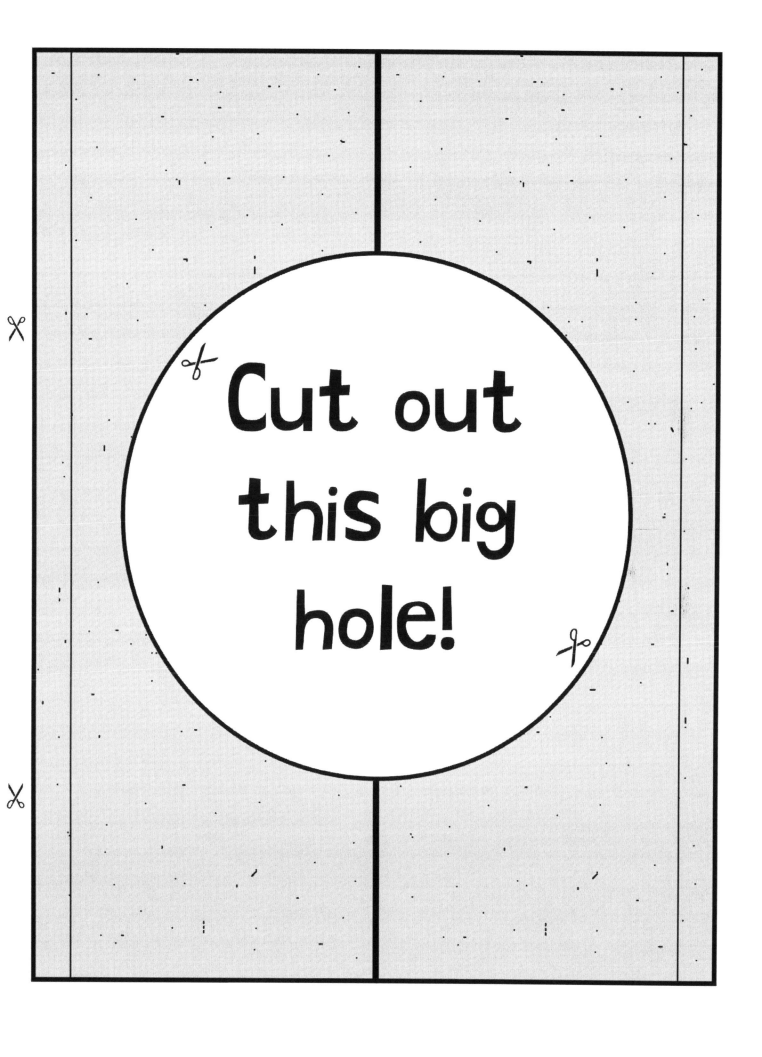

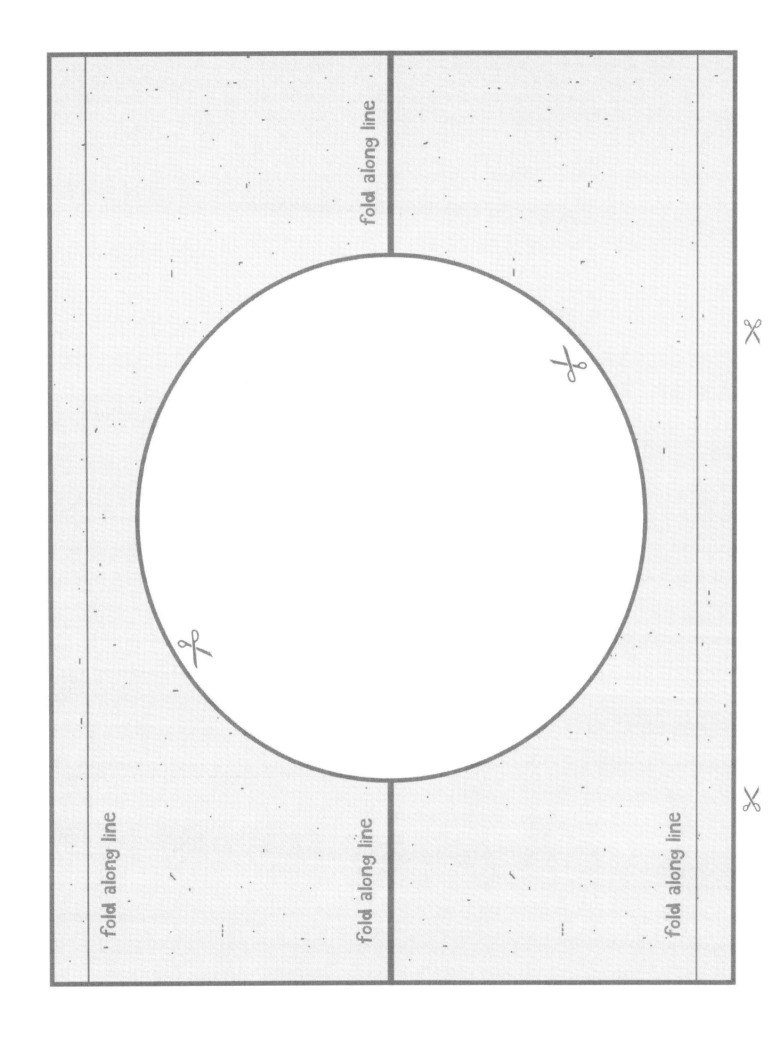

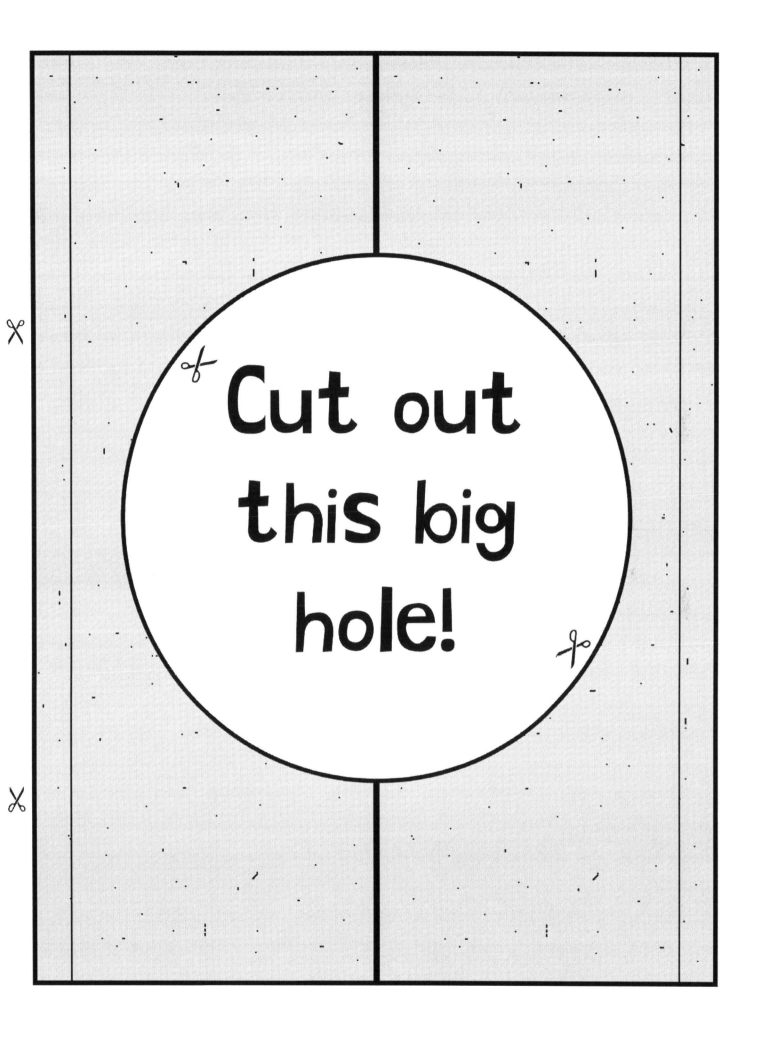

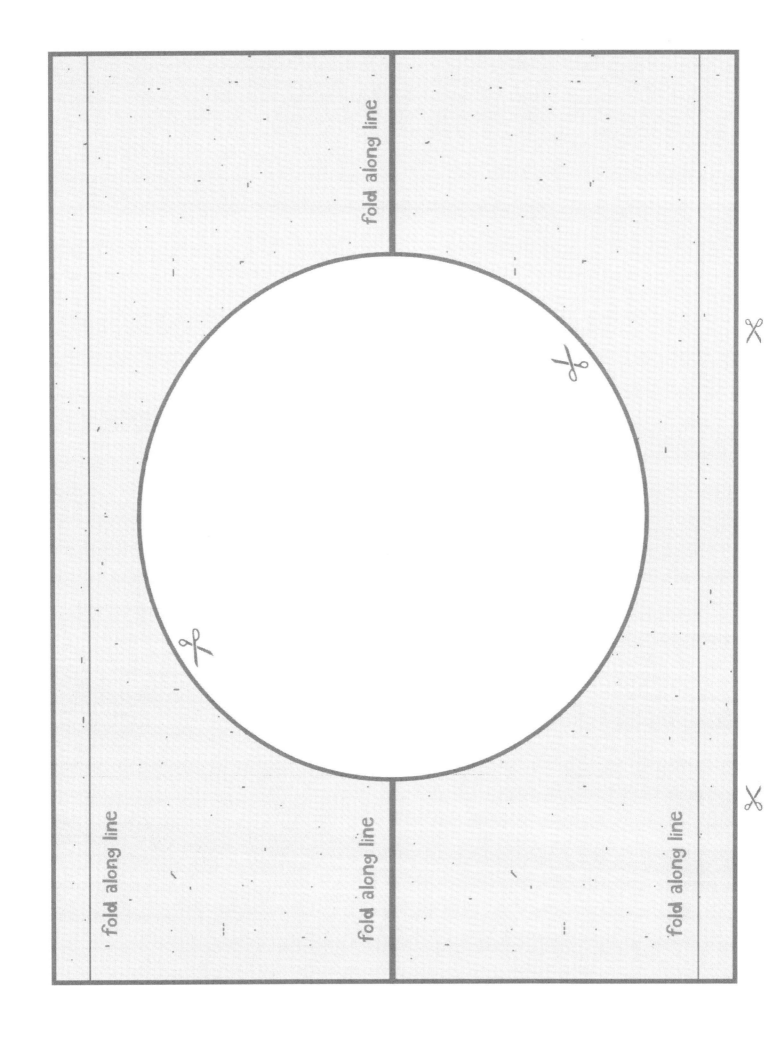

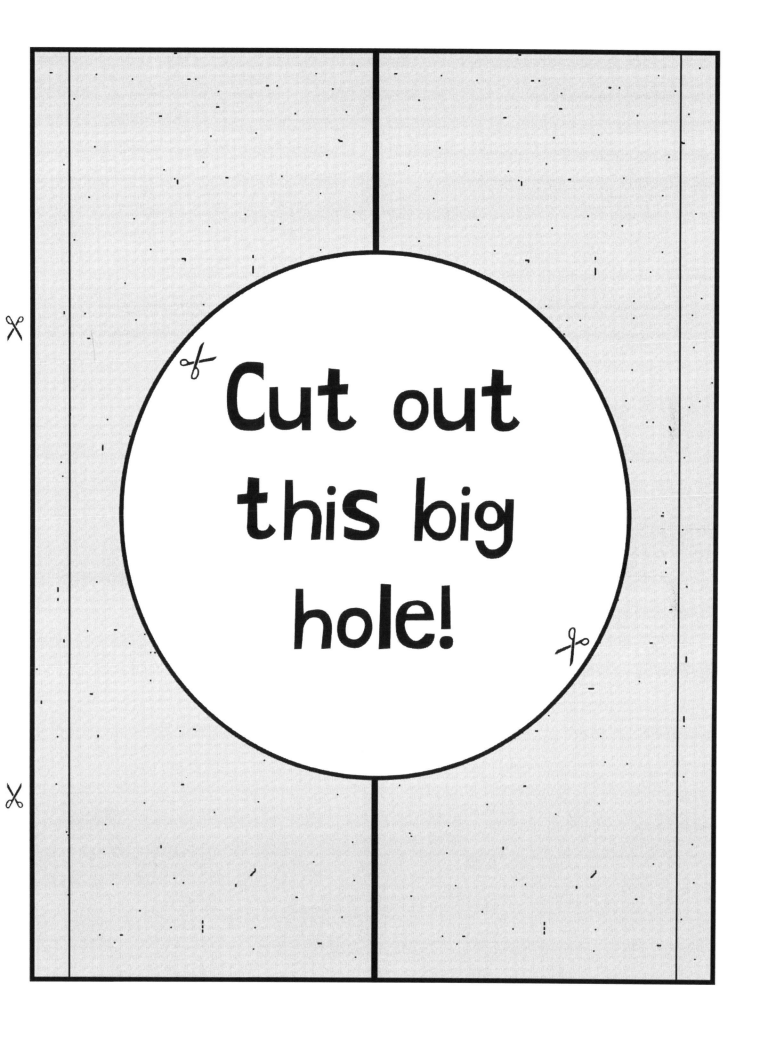

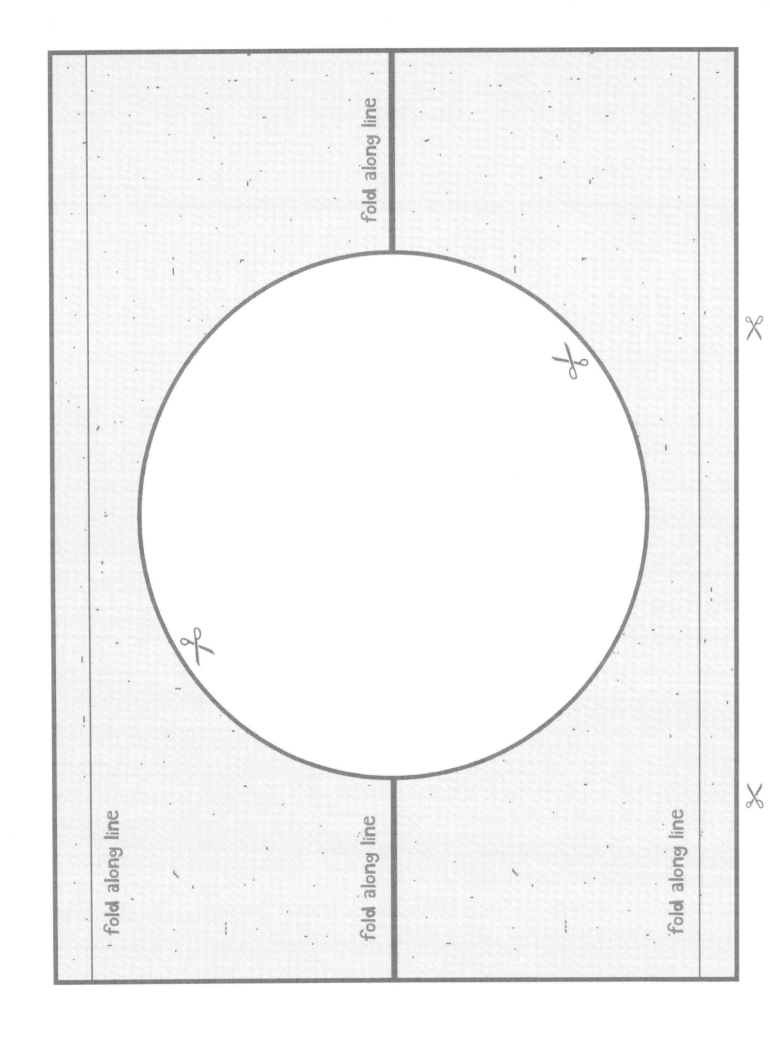

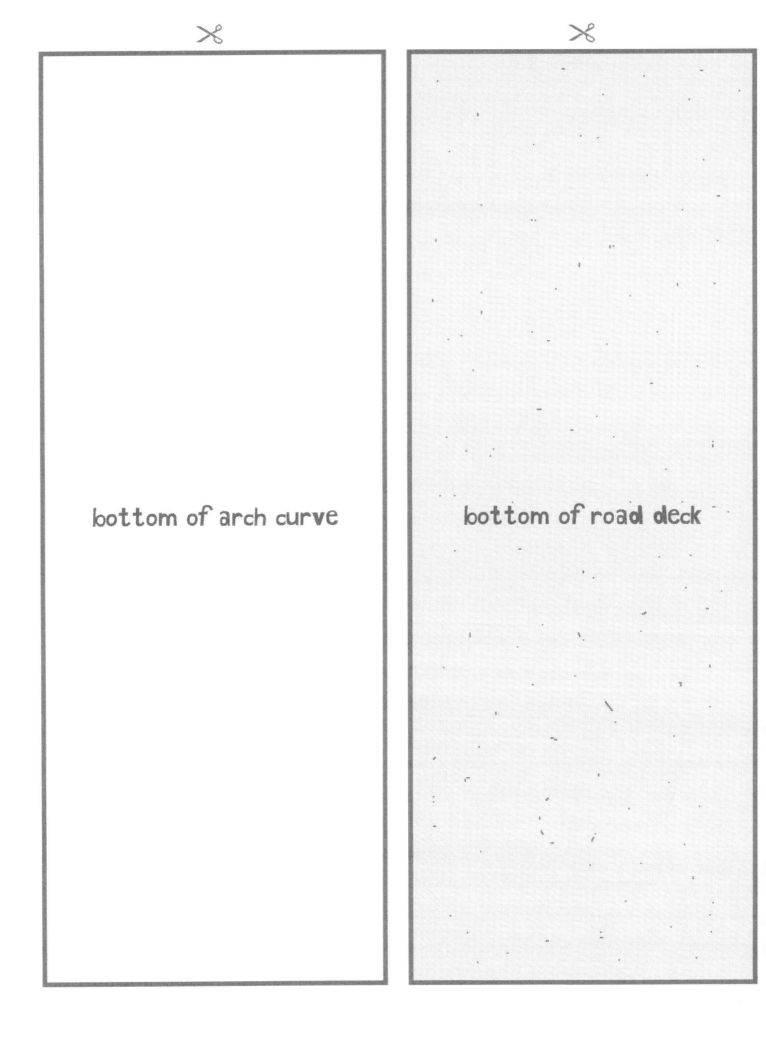

bottom of arch curve

bottom of road deck

CABLE STAYED BRIDGE

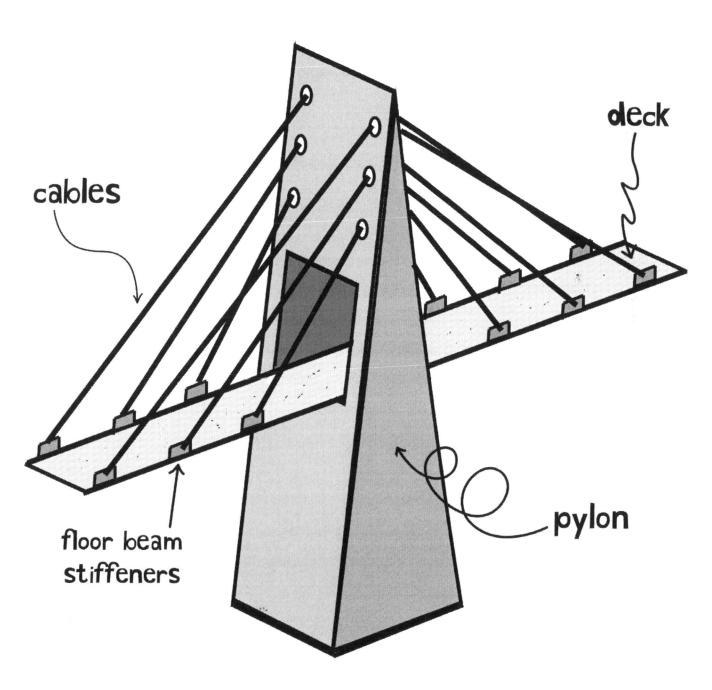

deck

cables

floor beam
stiffeners

pylon

How do they dig in water?

When they start a bridge, they put steel walls up and make a box to the floor of the body of water. Then they pump the water out. After that, they put in the piles and build the pylon on top. When they are done, the steel walls are pulled out.

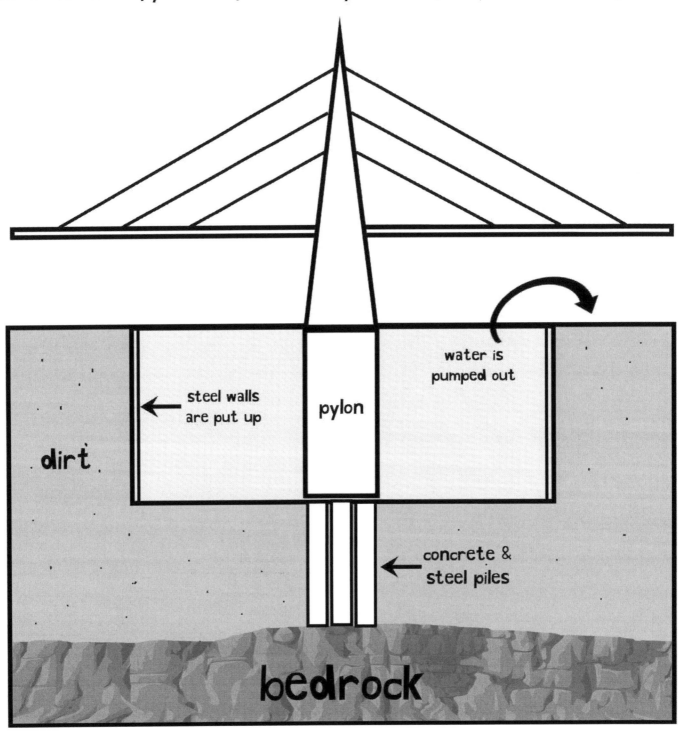

Concrete & steel tubes called "piles" go all the way down to the bedrock to make the pylon stand strong.

The Difference Between Suspension & Cable Stayed Bridges

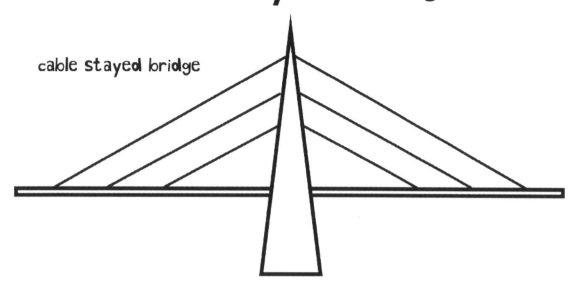

cable stayed bridge

The cables are connected directly from the pylon to the deck. These guys are less expensive to build but do not span as far as suspension bridges.

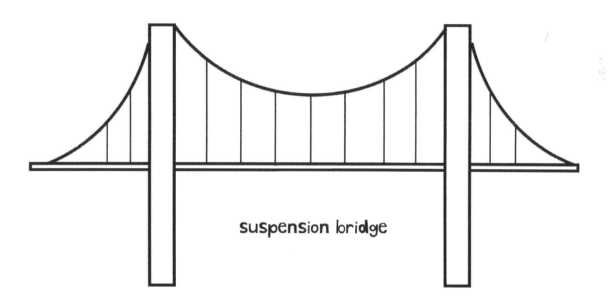

suspension bridge

For suspension bridges, there are big cables hung from the towers to anchors on both sides of the bridge. Then, smaller cables hang from the big cables to the deck. This allows for a long span, but these guys are expensive to build.

1.

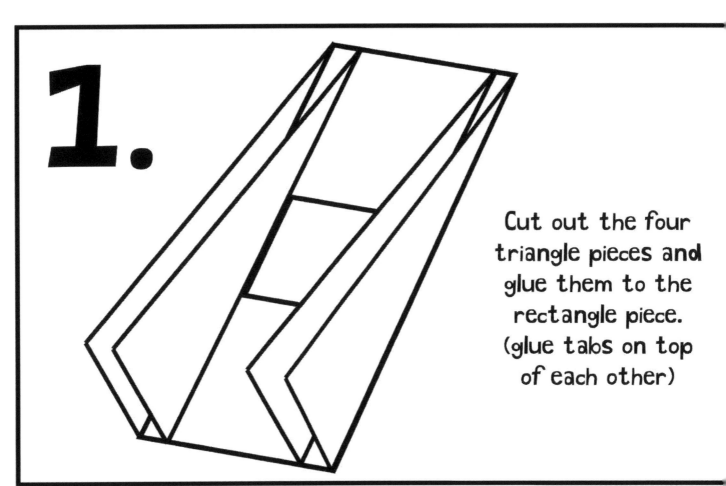

Cut out the four triangle pieces and glue them to the rectangle piece. (glue tabs on top of each other)

Cut out and glue the second rectangle piece on top.

2.

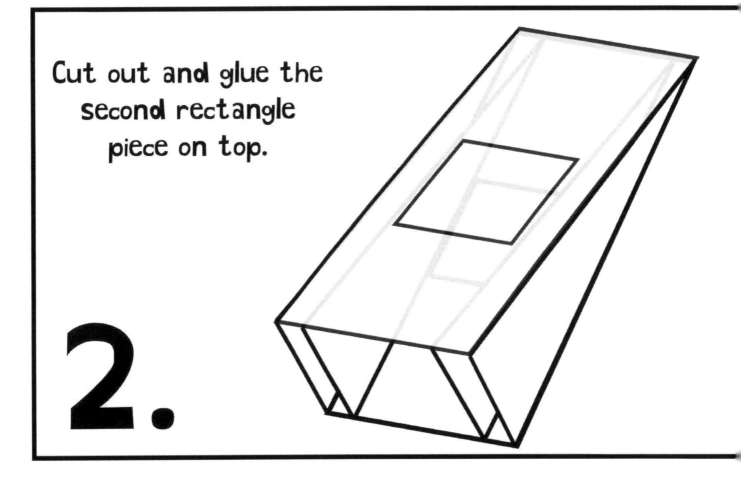

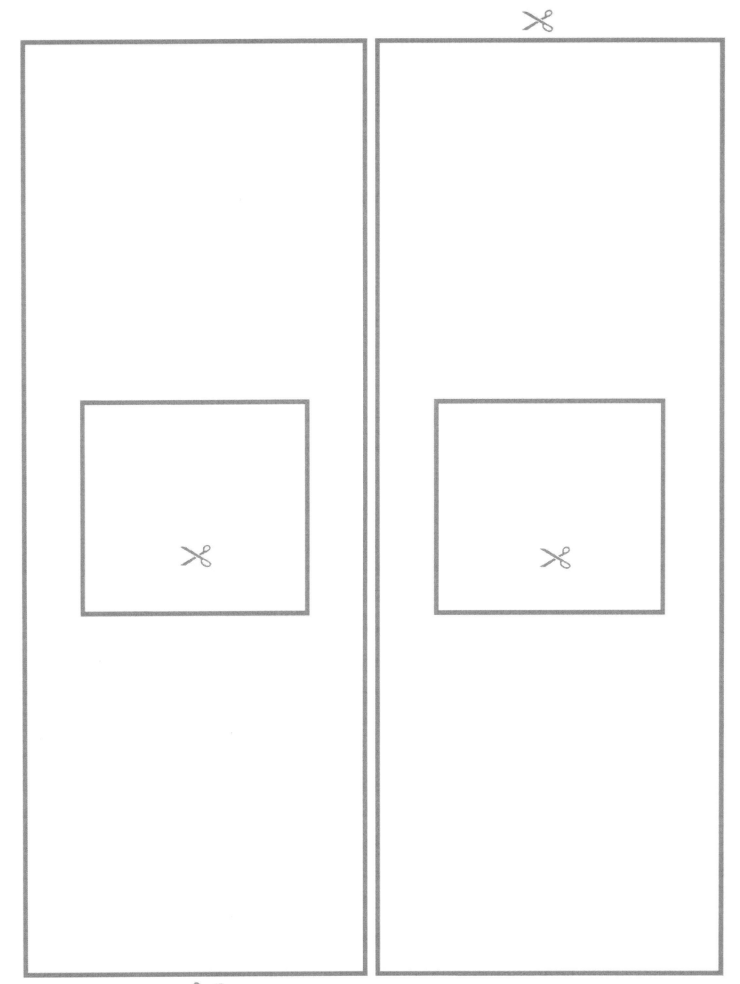

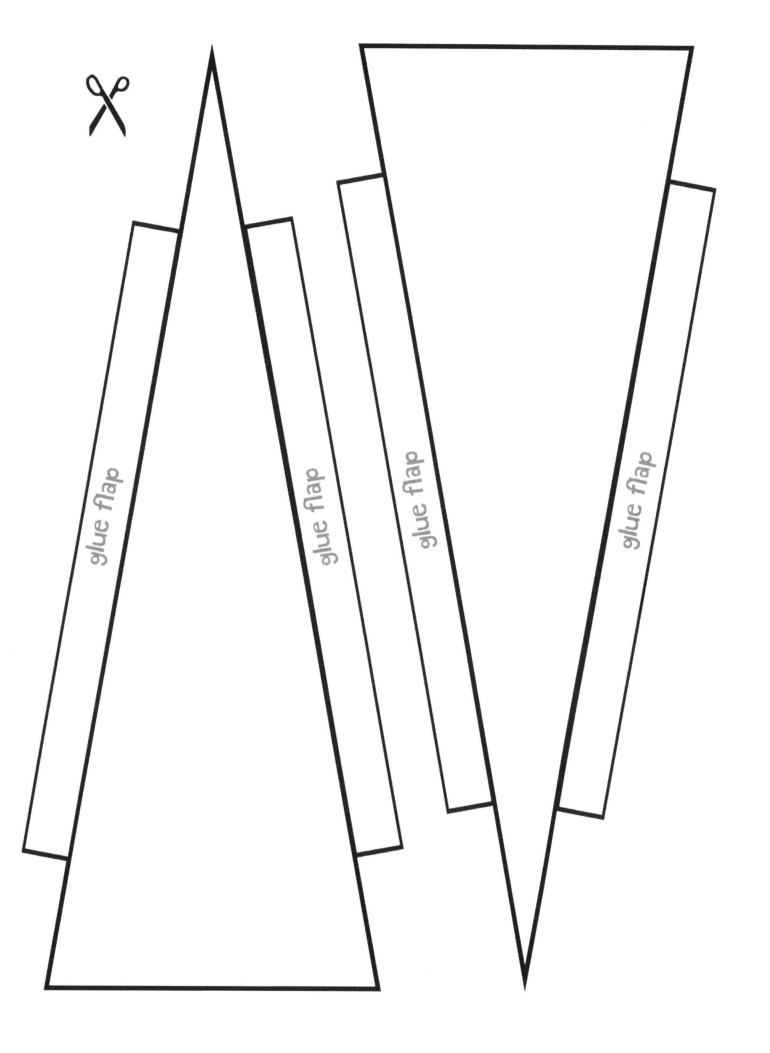

glue flap

glue flap

glue flap

glue flap

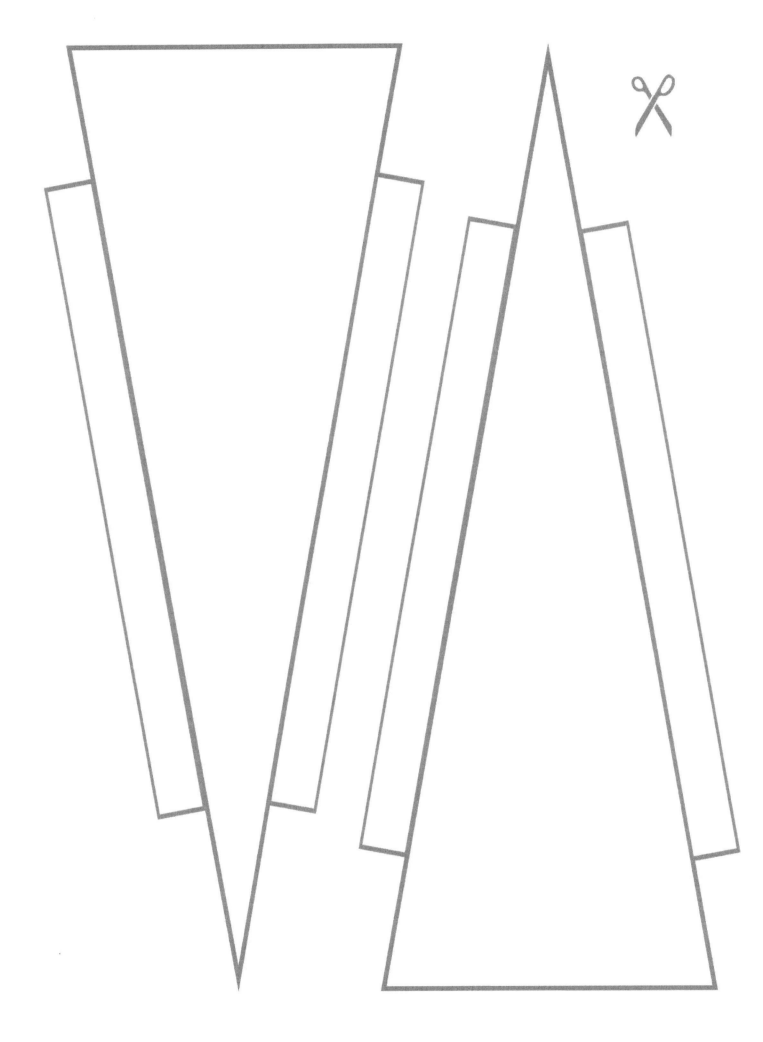

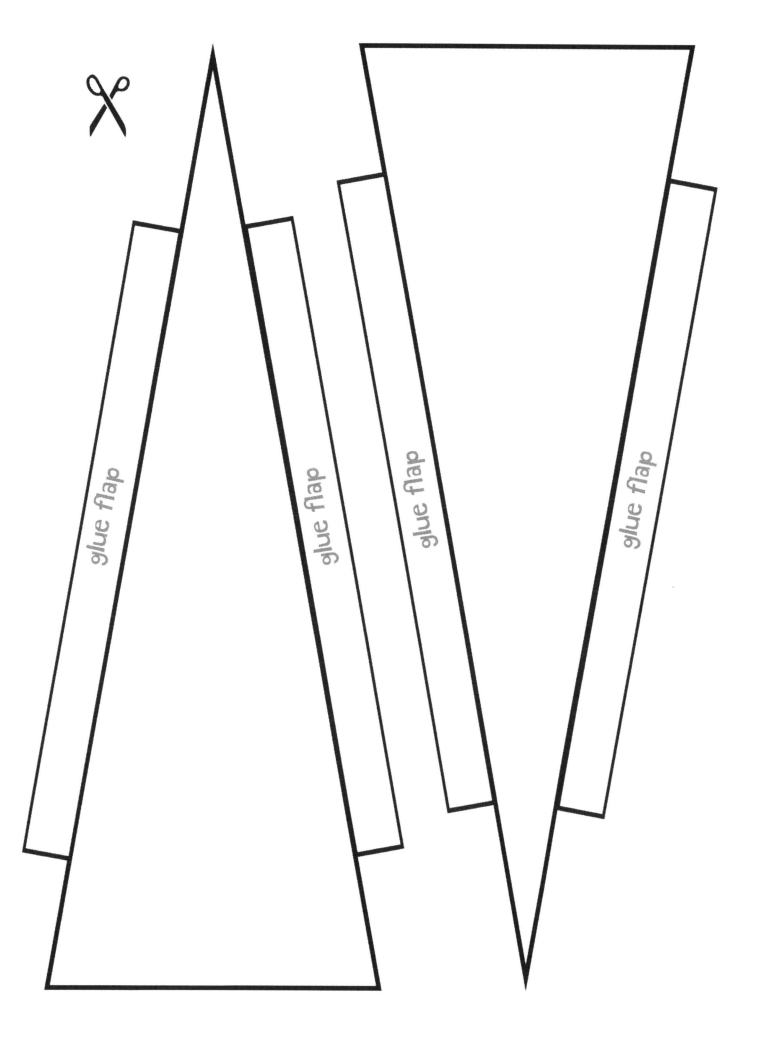

glue flap

glue flap

glue flap

glue flap

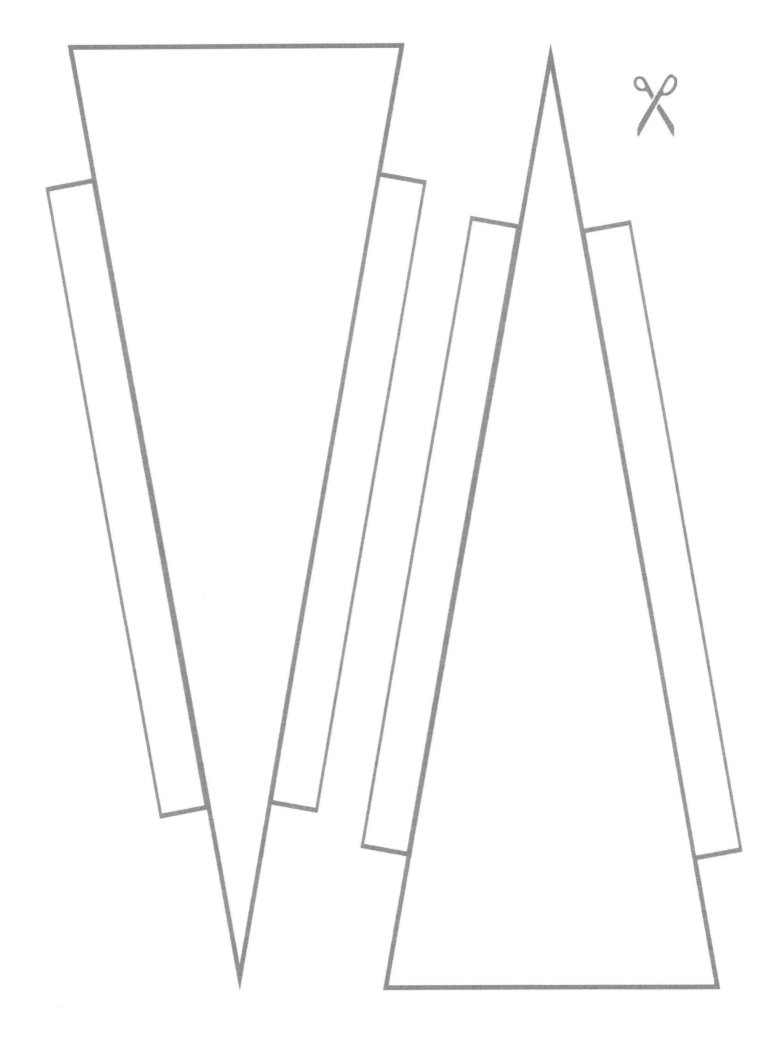

How is the deck built on a cable stayed bridge?

I am glad you asked. The road for a cable stayed bridge is built in sections. Starting from the middle and adding pieces on both sides 'till they reach the end. Each side balances out the other. Kind of like a scale.

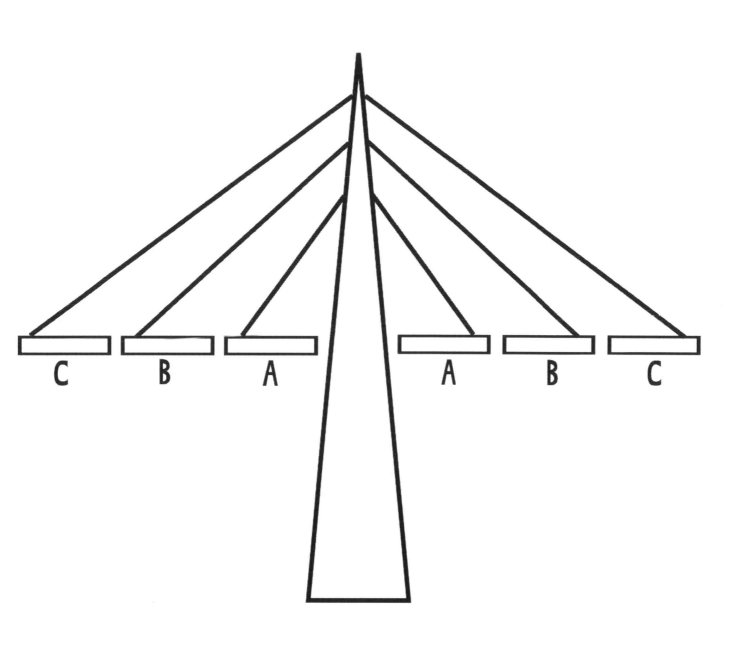

1.

Cut out, fold, and glue the road deck flat.

Cut out, fold, and glue the six deck beams flat. Fold on line.

2.

Glue floor beams on the lines of the white side of road deck.

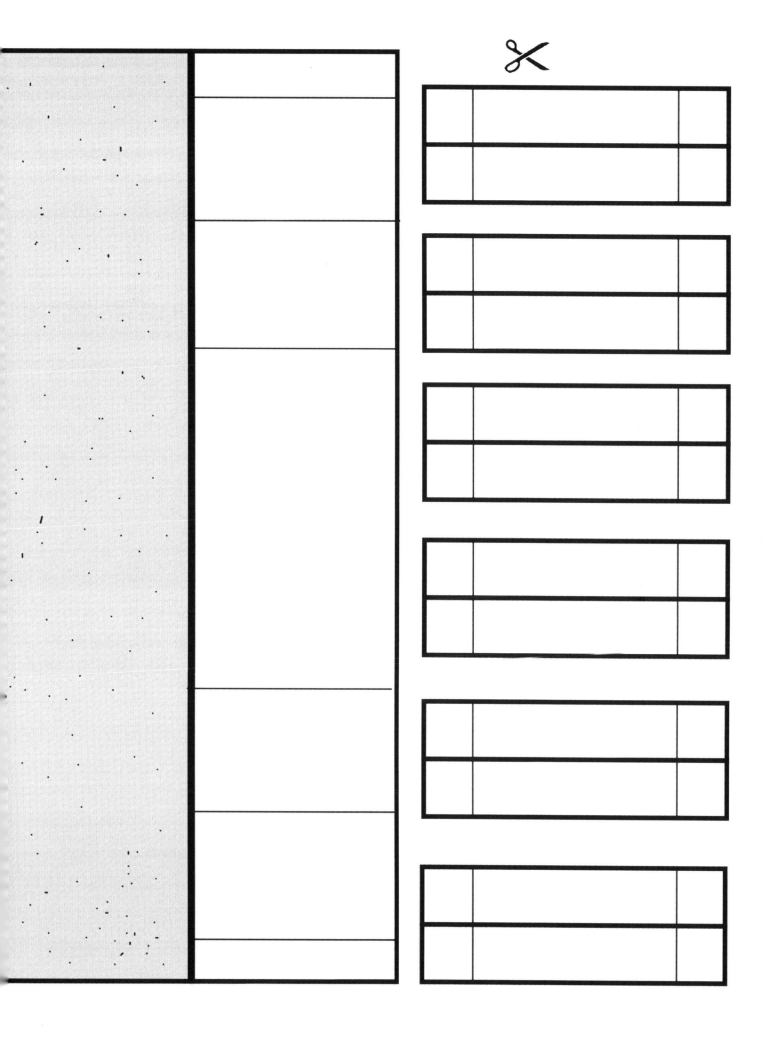

deck floor beam 1

deck floor beam 2

deck floor beam 3

deck floor beam 4

deck floor beam 5

deck floor beam 6

fold on line

deck

CABLE ANCHORS

The cables of a cable stayed bridge are made of steel and are very strong, but they have to be held down to something. That's where cable anchors come into play. The cable is pulled tight and fastened securely to the anchor.

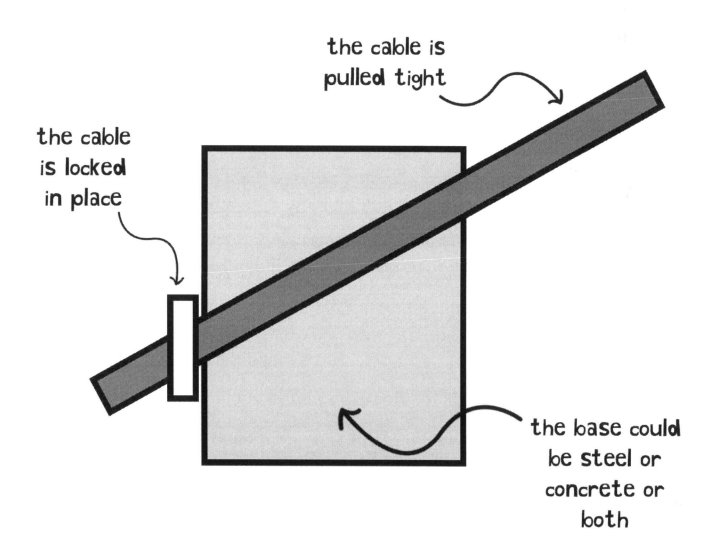

the cable is pulled tight

the cable is locked in place

the base could be steel or concrete or both

Use a pencil and roll the twelve cable strips diagonally until they make a long thin tube. Pull tight and tape or glue the ends.

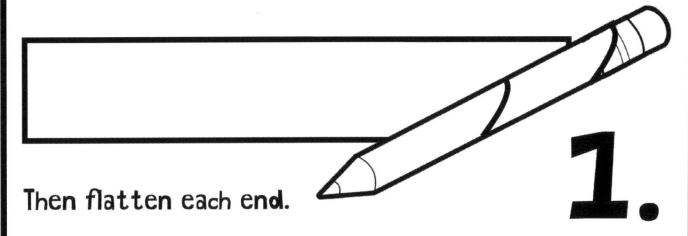

Then flatten each end.

1.

Glue the flatten ends on the circles on the pylon and then glue the other end to the floor beams like this.

2.

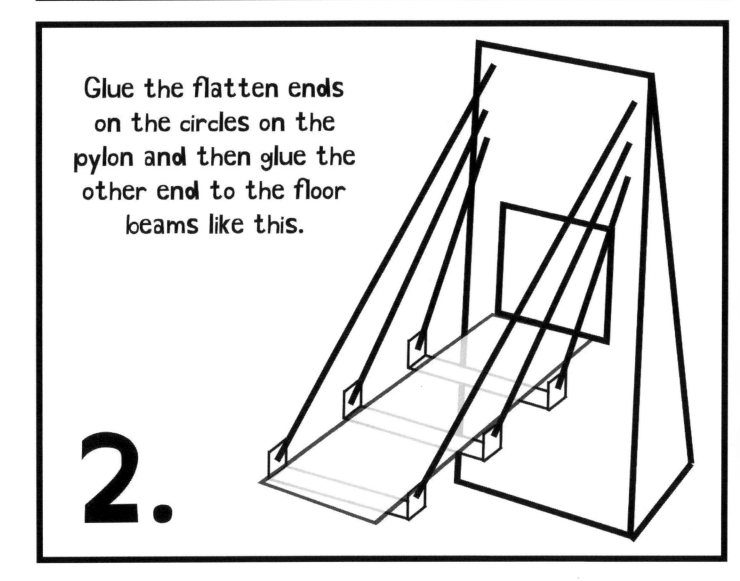

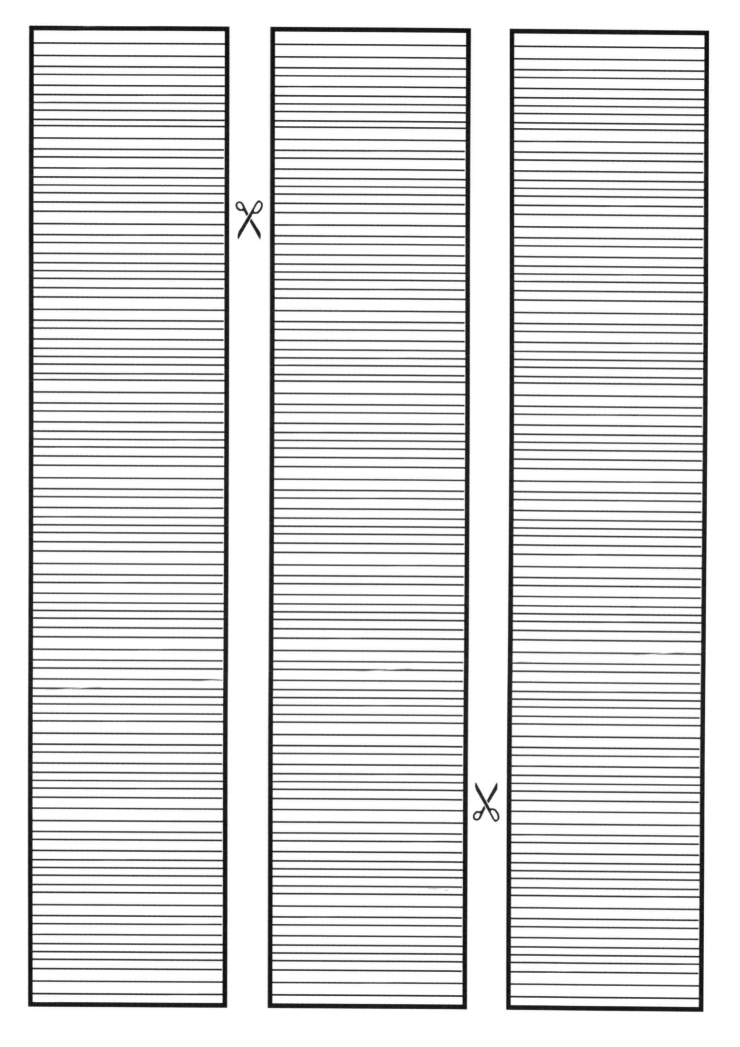

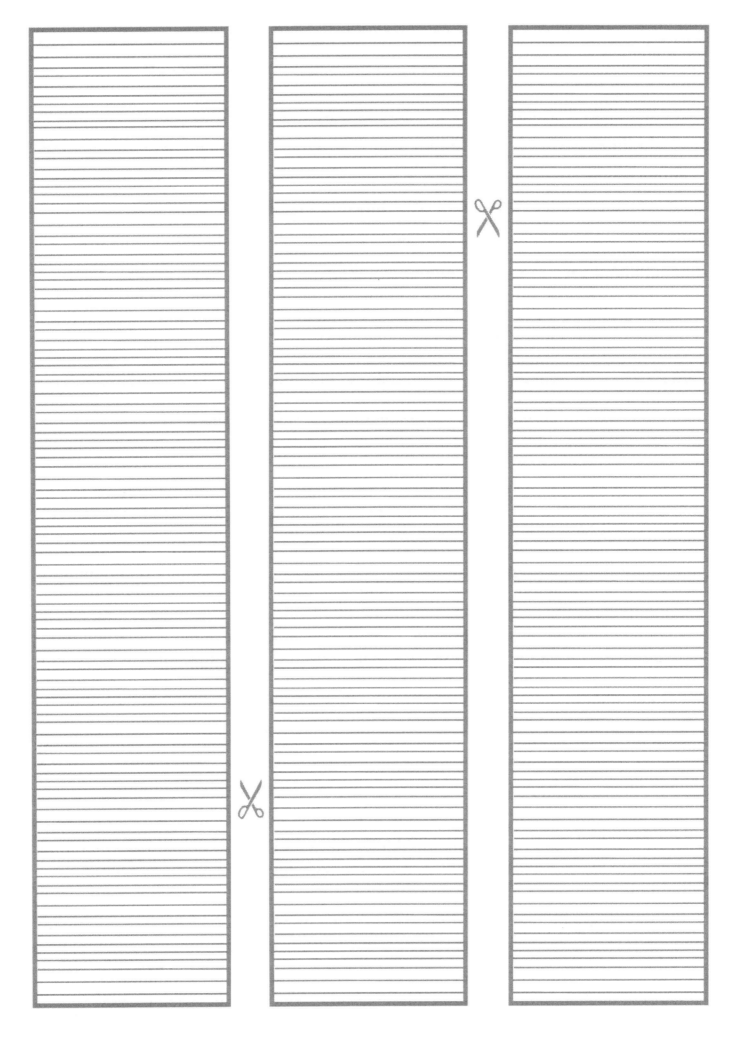

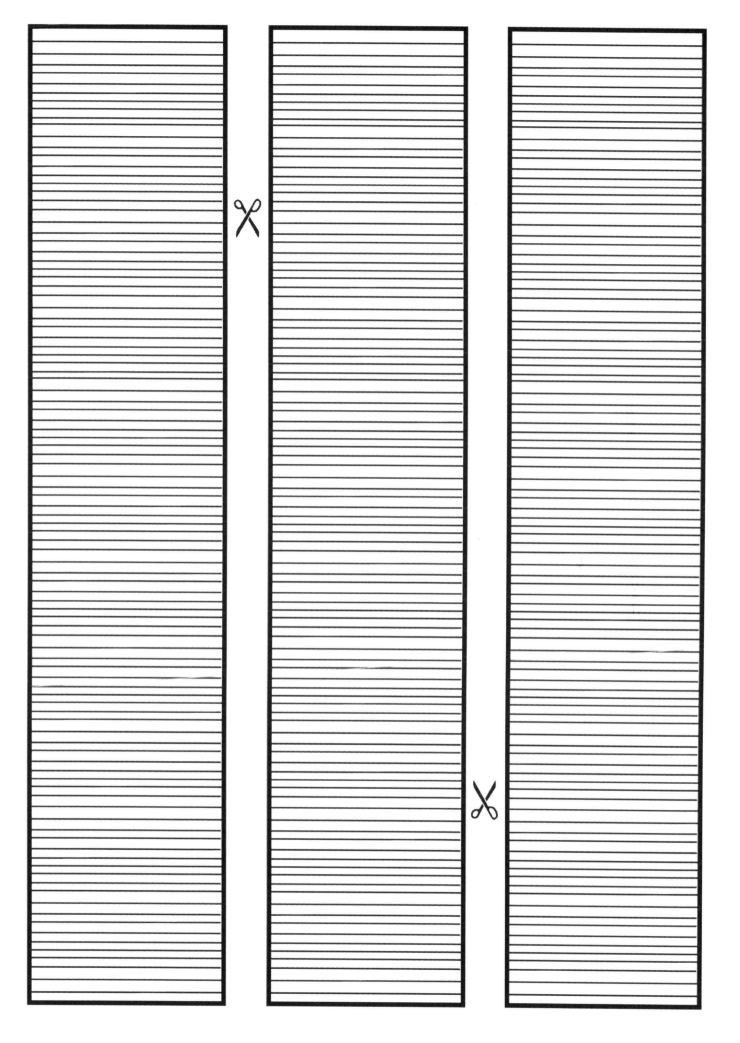

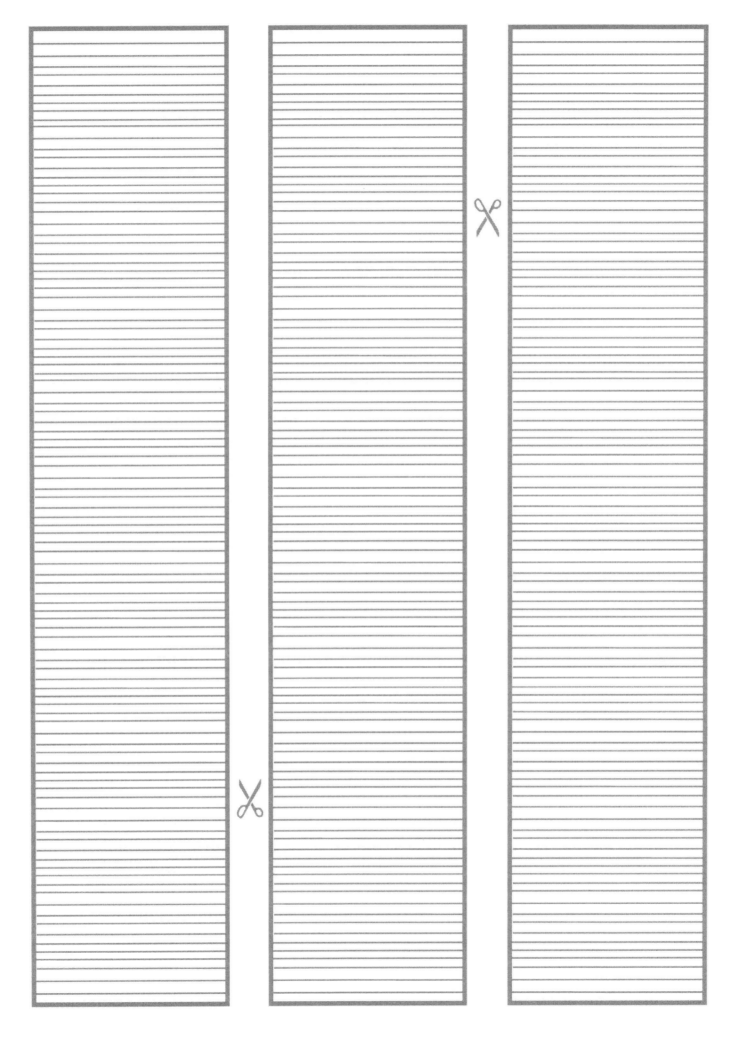

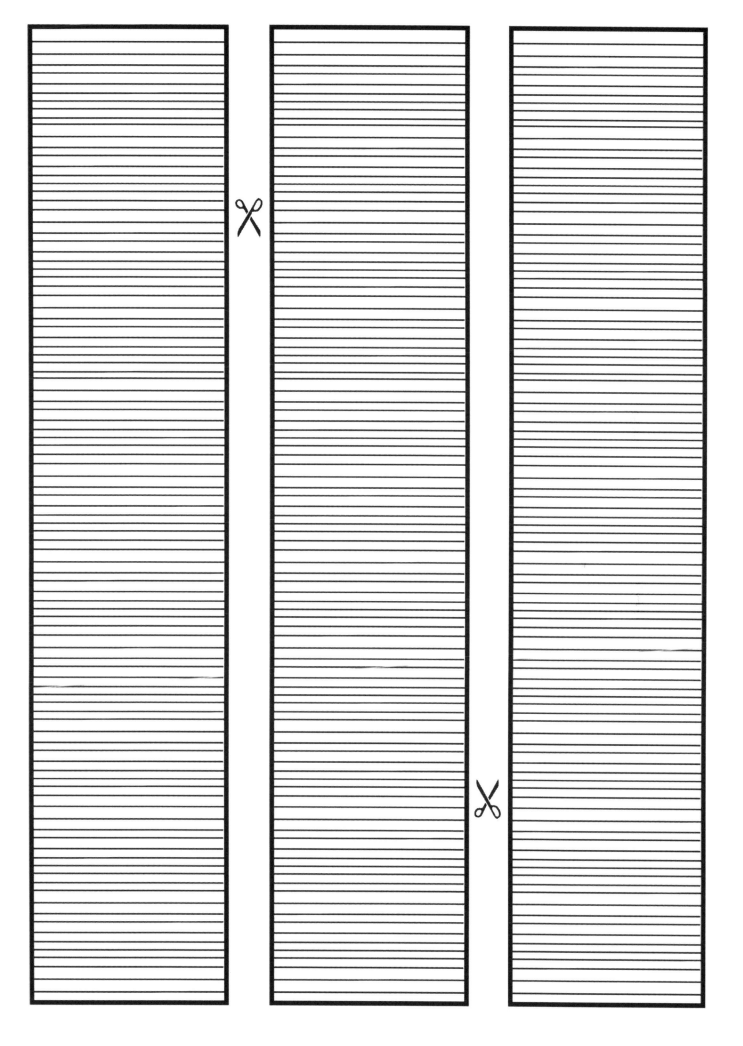

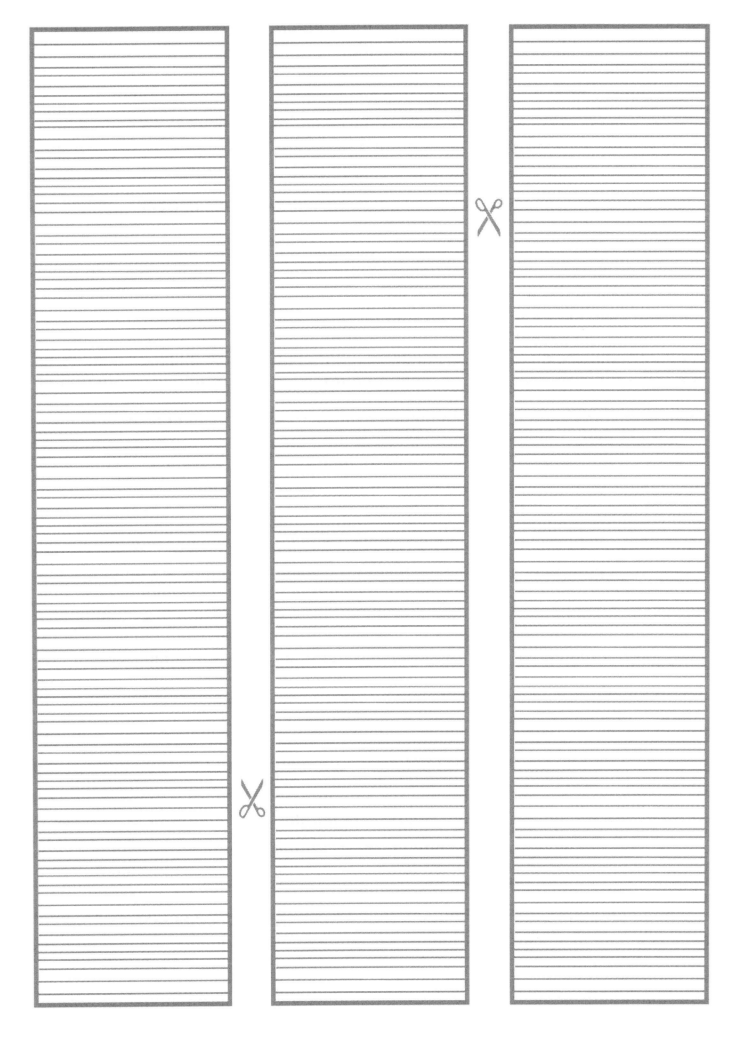

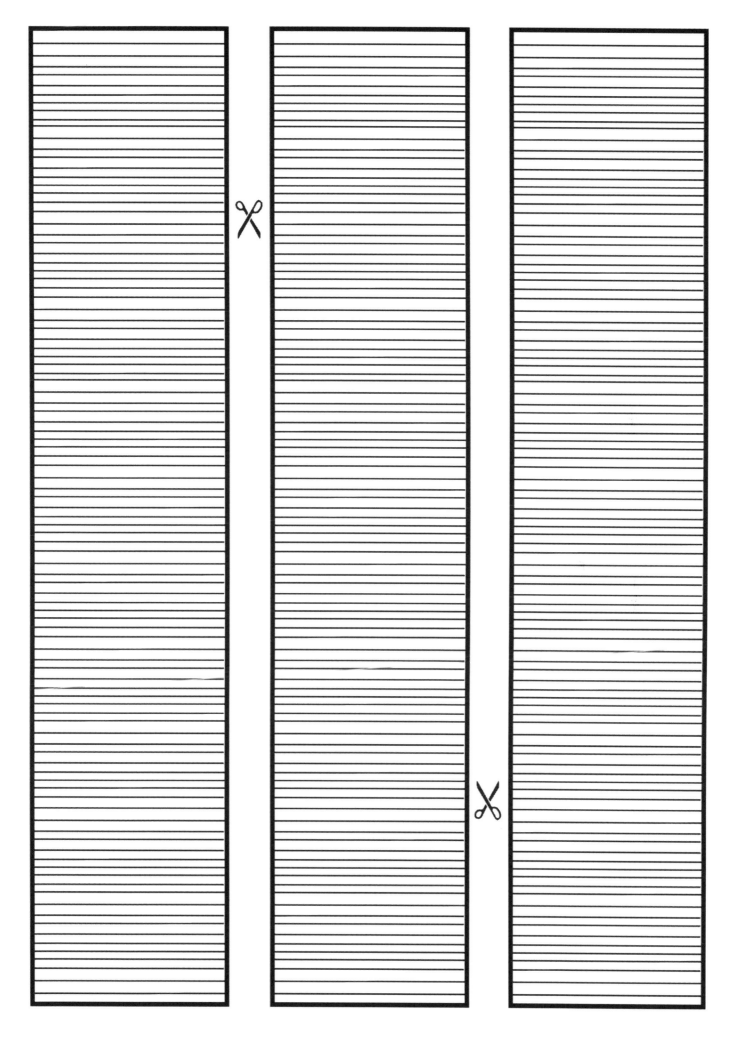

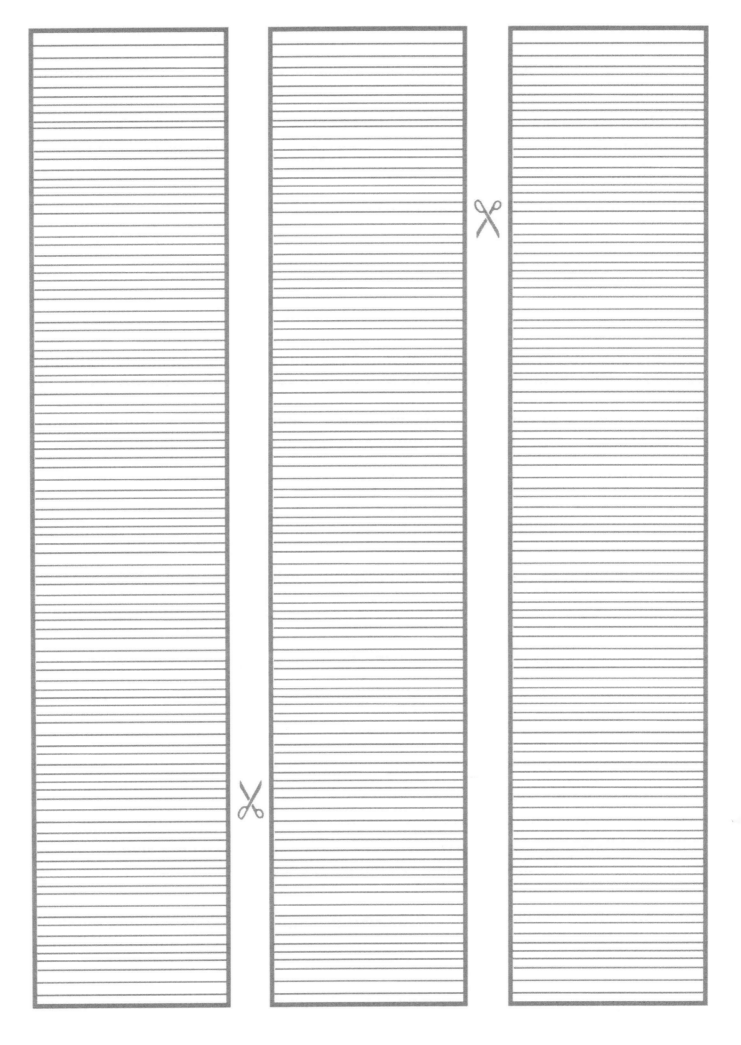

LET'S TEST OUR BRIDGES

Engineers are always testing things to find out how they can improve their designs. Let's test our paper bridges. We're gonna need something like two stacks of books of equal height to put our bridges on. Then we need some weight. Coins work nicely! We can load up the bridges with coins to see which bridge is the strongest and then record our results on the next page.

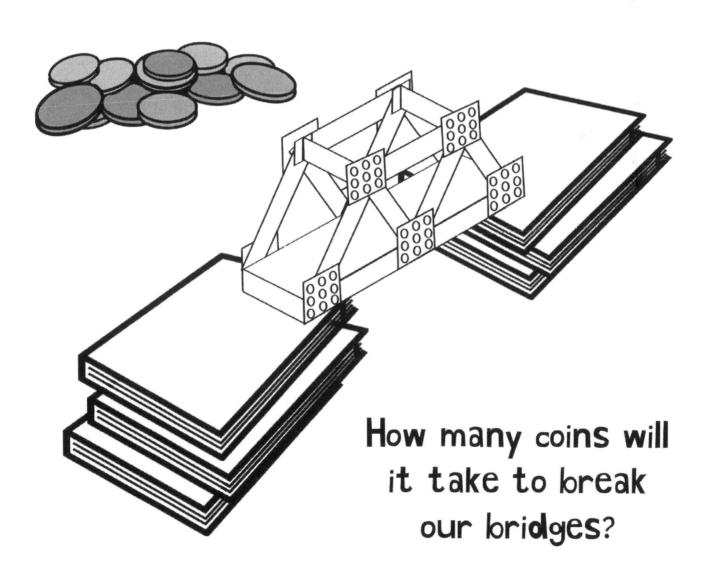

How many coins will it take to break our bridges?

BRIDGE TEST RESULTS

BRIDGE NAME	HOW MANY COINS TO BREAK IT	WHERE IT BROKE	I COULD MAKE IT STRONGER BY

HOPE
YOU SAVED THE
SCRAP
PAPER

MAKE YOU OWN DESIGN

With the scrap paper and your new knowledge on how some types of bridges work, try making your own design and then test it. GET CRAZY! Don't hold back! Remember IT'S ONLY PAPER!!!

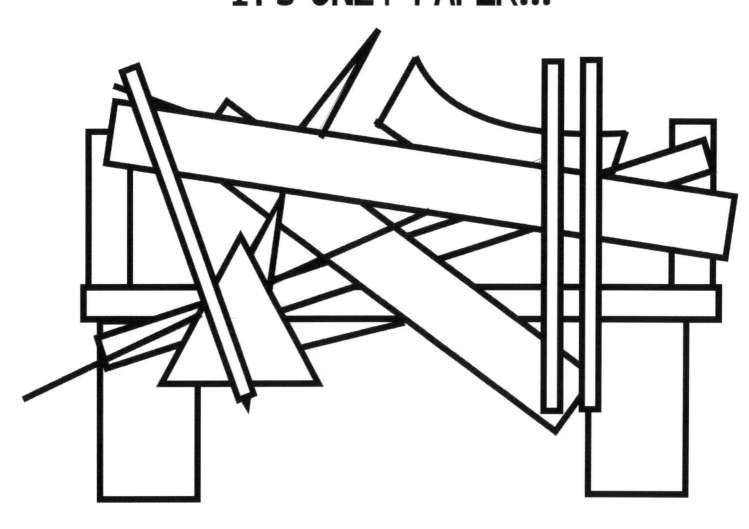

FIRST CLASS BRIDGE BUILDER

This is to certify that

Has passed everything with flying colors to become the best maker, designer, colorer, drawer, folder, logger, kid in the whole universe and is properly certified to be a:

PAPER BRIDGE ENGINEER WITH HONORS

VERIFIED BY: _____ DATE: _____

MORE BOOKS FROM THE SQUID

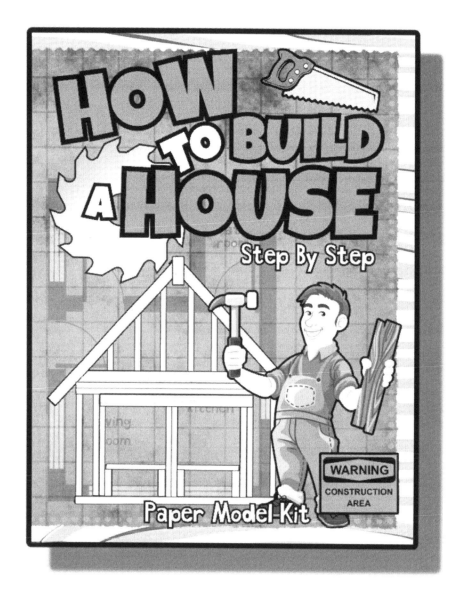

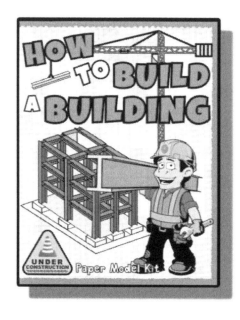

CHECK US OUT

ABOUT THE AUTHOR

ALBERT B. SQUID

HAS ANYONE SEEN THIS DUDE?

Born to a family of construction peeps, ALBERT B. SQUID was raised on construction sites in Massachusetts. Believe it or not, he holds two degrees in Engineering and Architecture and has worked as an Architect in Boston, Tokyo, and Seoul. In the year 2000, Squid started an independent children's book publishing company in NYC. I had fun doing that.....I mean HE (Albert B. Squid) had fun doing that! After becoming a freelance voice actor, the elusive author's whereabouts are unknown. He was last spotted with a leg injury on a ship going to Boston. I guess you could say he was shipping up to ......Who Knows!

Printed in Great Britain
by Amazon

71940518R00050